Remembering Malcolm

Remembering Malcolm

by Benjamin Karim
with Peter Skutches & David Gallen

Carroll & Graf Publishers, Inc.
New York

Copyright © 1992 by Benjamin Karim, Peter Skutches,
and David Gallen

First Carroll & Graf edition 1992

Carroll & Graf Publishers, Inc.
260 Fifth Avenue
New York, NY 10001

Library of Congress Cataloging-in-Publication Data

Karim, Benjamin.
    Remembering Malcolm ; the story of Malcolm X from
inside the Muslim mosque by his assistant minister,
Benjamin Karim / by Benjamin Karim with Peter
Skutches & David Gallen. — 1st Carroll & Graf ed.
        p.   cm.
    Includes index.
    ISBN 0-88184-901-4 : $21.00. — ISBN 0-88184-881-6 :
$10.95
    1. X, Malcolm, 1925–1965.   2. Karim, Benjamin.
3. Black Muslims—Biography.   4. Afro-Americans—
Biography.   I. Gallen, David.   II. Skutches, Peter.
III. Title.
BP223.Z8L575   1992
320.5′4′092—dc20
    [B]   92-38607
                                                      CIP

I dedicate this book to the memory of my late grand-mother, Sarah, and parents, Maryam and Wilbur, and to my wonderful family—to my wife, Linda; my children, Zaid, Tariq, Jamal, Jahlil, Khadijah, Asia; my grandchildren, Zirchi, Vashti, Maryam Neri, Talite, Zaki; and the mothers of my grandchildren, Valencia, Kim, and Sherri.

Acknowledgments

To David Gallen and Peter Skutches I extend my special thanks. Without them my memories would not have become a manuscript.

Several times over the past few years various publishers had approached me regarding the possibility of writing a memoir about my association with Malcolm X, but I had always been a little wary. Then, in August 1991, I met David Gallen. I was impressed by his sincerity and absolute honesty, and I was encouraged to explore my memory for the man that I had known as Brother Minister. A series of marathon interviews with David sometimes tried the patience and shortened the tempers of us both, but for the most part our work together brought us pleasure—and ultimately satisfaction.

With Peter Skutches, who coauthored the manuscript, eight years of experience, a lifetime of feelings, and hours upon hours of thoughts and memories were shaped into the story that unfolds in the pages of this book.

1934

A race of devils—white devils, blue-eyed devils—now rules the world. Their days, though, are numbered, for the time of Armageddon is nigh. Then will fire sear the earth and blood drench the land. In the wilderness of North America the oppressor shall meet his doom; the evil white enemy will fall ignominiously into destruction while in the East the black Muslims shall rise triumphant to rule forever in freedom, justice, and equality the planet Earth. A New World Order will be born.

Images of Armageddon figured significantly in the sermons of Brother Minister Malcolm X at Harlem's Temple Number Seven in the late 1950s, and no doubt the word that the earth would be restored by Allah to the Islamic faithful in the aftermath of this final battle against the forces of evil was also heard in the Chicago mosque where Elijah Muhammad, the One True Messenger (so he was called), headed the Nation of Islam for forty-one years. The message, however, was first delivered by a man named Fard.

W.D. Fard sold dry goods. He purveyed hope, too. Like many a drummer and traveling man, Fard seemed to have come from nowhere. Indeed, you might think he had simply materialized out of a bank of clouds tumbling on the horizon of a wide, midwestern, black-and-white movie sky as into the camera's eye you might imagine he drives a wagon, or does he ride the wind? His sleek hair is blown back, and his eyes

7

are dark and fiery. A tarp billows up behind him; beneath it, in bolts or in carpetbags, jostle his fabulous wares. A squall of dust marks his path through the open fields. Frame houses paled by harsh winters and now by the summer sun begin to punctuate the thirsty land. A city lies within his sight.

W.D. Fard arrived in Detroit late in the summer of 1930. From door to door in the city's black ghetto, as Louis Lomax tells the tale in *When the Word Is Given*, Fard peddled his wares, satins and silks like those worn by regal blacks in Africa, so he eloquently claimed. Talker though he was, Fard hawked no cure-alls, promised no miracles in bottles of snake oil. He did, however, tender ointment for the oppressed soul. Into lives embittered by the northern ghetto and further impoverished by the Depression he brought glimpses of distant, more romantic lands. He spoke of his travels in the Near East and adventures in the Orient. He spoke of a pilgrimage to Mecca, and from the Holy City of Islam he brought a message. He spoke, and an eager audience listened.

From the outset mystery shrouded Fard—or Farrad Mohammad or Mr. F.M. Ali or Professor Ford or Wali Farrad, as he was variously known. His complexion, paler than dusky, suggested to some an Arabian prince; many believed he came from Palestine, and others said India. Or he may have been born into the tribe of Koreish like the founder of traditional Islam, Muhammad himself. One report held that he had abandoned a diplomatic career in London to fulfill the more compelling mission of awakening black people in America to their noble history and thus freeing them from their white oppressors. Whatever, according to Lomax, he soon became known as the Prophet, and his fearless words, his fervent assault on the "white devils," began to attract crowds too large for meetings in the small rooms of slum dwellings. Fard's followers hired a hall; it was called the Temple of Islam, and a black Muslim movement had been born.

Fard's following grew. Institutionalization set in. Lomax points out that new members had to meet strict requirements for admittance; examinations had to be passed, moral commitments honored, monetary pledges met. A University of Islam was established for the elementary and high-school education of Muslim children. Muslim Girls Training classes instructed Muslim women in the arts of proper Muslim housekeeping and motherhood. The paramilitary Fruit of Islam schooled Muslim men in judo and the use of firearms. Fard himself produced two fundamental theological texts for the movement: *The Sacred Ritual of the Nation of Islam* and the cryptic *Teachings for the Lost Found Nation of Islam in a Mathematical Way*.

Shortly after Fard arrived in Detroit he met Elijah Poole. The son of a Baptist minister and slave, Poole had left rural Georgia with his wife and children in 1923 to pursue the economic promise of the industrial North. He was then twenty-six; seven years later he was jobless, bitter, disillusioned, poor. And ready for W.D. Fard. Poole attended one of Fard's house meetings, as Lomax recounts it, and immediately they became friends. In 1932 Poole was designated the first Chief Minister of Islam by Fard, who further elevated Poole's status by bestowing upon him the much coveted name of Muhammad. In 1934 Chief Minister Elijah Muhammad assumed the leadership of the Nation of Islam and relocated its national headquarters to Temple Number Two in Chicago. He also declared Fard divine and named him the Prophet of Allah.

The Prophet himself had vanished. As mysteriously as he had appeared among the disenchanted in Detroit's city slums Fard had left their midst—perhaps on some rumored voyage to Europe, perhaps at the shadowy hands of Detroit's white police, or maybe by the foul play of Muslim malcontents. It has been said, too, that he may have been offered up to Allah as a human sacrifice. The leaden city sky held no answer.

In 1934, not eighty miles from Detroit, in East Lansing,

Michigan, Malcolm Little turned nine. His father, Earl Little, a Baptist preacher and Garveyite involved in the "back to Africa" movement, had died three years earlier when he had fallen in the path of a moving streetcar. (Rumor had it that Little had been first murdered by the Black Legion, a local white supremacist group, and then thrown onto the streetcar tracks.) Fatherless, Malcolm's family was doubly bereft, for the Depression continued to erode the Littles' pride and resources. *The Autobiography of Malcolm X* poignantly describes how day after day of that bleak year 1934 Louise Little, Malcolm's mother, would boil a big pot of dandelion greens to feed her eleven children, all of them dizzy from hunger, and daily they would be taunted by neighborhood kids for eating "fried grass." On luckier days they would eat cornmeal mush.

And across three state lines to the south and east of Michigan, in Suffolk, Virginia, in 1934 Benjamin Karim was two.

Six Hundred Miles from Lansing

Malcolm Little understood hunger. In many ways it defined his childhood. Certainly it taught him lessons he would never forget, and years later Malcolm X would be lecturing his assistant minister Benjamin Karim on hunger as the most basic of human drives.

Not only did Malcolm in his boyhood suffer the pangs of physical hunger for want of food; he also sharply experienced hunger for affection, acceptance, guidance, encouragement. The Littles lived meagerly, and more and more the economic hardships of the Depression drained Louise Little's emotional and spiritual reserves. She became despondent, withdrew from harsh realities. By 1937 the Little family was rapidly deteriorating. Malcolm had begun stealing. He was twelve when he found himself in the first of what would be numerous foster homes. In January 1939, following a severe nervous breakdown, Malcolm's mother was declared legally insane and committed to the state mental hospital at Kalamazoo. Still, Malcolm himself clung to his diminished pride and his ambitions, continually battered though they were. As he relates in the *Autobiography*, one day he confided to his favorite eighth grade teacher that he wanted to be a lawyer, only to be told that "that's no realistic goal for a nigger"— even though Malcolm at the time was ranked near the top of his otherwise white class. That day marked a turning point for Malcolm, then thirteen. Within months he would be exploring the street life of Boston.

More than miles separated the childhood experience of Malcolm Little in the bleak northern suburbs of Lansing from that of Benjamin Karim in rural Suffolk, Virginia. Suffolk lies about eighty miles south of Richmond, and when Benjamin Karim was growing up in the 1930s, it was that small you could see from one end of the town to the other in an easy glance. By then Suffolk was feeling the economic pinch of the Great Depression, but still trade continued at the general store where townswomen bartered fresh eggs or homegrown poultry for provisions. In the barbershop men gathered for easy gossip or talked idly of the weather, crops, hard times. Kids kicked up the dust in quiet streets or played in the shade of fruit-bearing trees, or they helped to weed the vegetable patches planted in the backyards of small clapboard houses.

In one of those houses, on July 14, 1932, a midwife delivered the first, and only, child of young Mary Goodman in her mother Sarah's bed. The child was baptized Benjamin and given his mother's family name. (Not until 1978 did he take the Muslim name Karim.) In private Mary called him Dickieboy, a term of affection that would survive nearly twenty years, as would the inviolable bond forged by Mary with her son in his early childhood. It was a "good childhood," as Benjamin Karim remembers it, and he describes the small-town boy who grew up in the meager thirties as being "absolutely content." He recalls the simplicity of daily life then, and the sense of community that prompted people to help their neighbors and enabled them to rely on friends. And no matter how much his family may have wanted for material goods or a dollar's pleasures, they never wanted for food.

* * *

Everybody had gardens, *Benjamin Karim remembers.* We would grow corn and beans and onions and radishes, whatever, and in the summer the fruit trees would bury us in pears and apples. We'd pick wild berries, too. Then the women would put the fruit up in jars. They'd have big pots bubbling on the stove, all the fruit smelling as sweet as the season, and while they were cooking, we boys would be out back chopping wood to feed the stove. For days we'd keep the fire going, until we'd have hundreds of jars of fruit preserves and other home-canned goods—vegetables and sauces and relishes—stored out in the pantry. So in the wintertime nobody would have to worry about going hungry. We also had pigs, three or four of them, and we raised chickens, so we always had fresh eggs.

We didn't really need a lot of money. If we ran out of flour or sugar, say, we would gather up a few eggs and take them to Mr. Nichols's general store. Two or three eggs might bring us enough pennies to buy a pound of flour or as much of sugar, and that's a nice taste of sugar. One of our chickens, dressed, would get us both the flour and the sugar and maybe some rice or potatoes as well as a nickel soda for me. We bartered like that quite a bit. Or we borrowed. Neighbors helped each other out with a scoop of flour or cup of milk; what we had we shared. We've lost communal values like that, like we've lost our fruit trees and farming land to real-estate developers. You'd have to search hard to find the Suffolk I knew as a child.

Suffolk was divided by railroad tracks. White people lived on one side of the tracks and on the other lived the blacks. For a time we lived right by the railroad tracks. Day and night the trains would be running past my grandmother's house, where we lived, but they really didn't bother us; they just told us what time it was. On either side of the railroad tracks lay a drainage ditch, and sometimes some of us black kids would cross the near ditch and the railroad tracks and then the ditch opposite, or else the white kids would cross

from their side—they'd be the poor white kids, the ones who
lived near the tracks—and we'd play together. We'd play
childhood street games or run wild in the woods. We had
fun, and I don't remember a single fight ever between us, not
when we were little kids.

My grandmother worked for a family in the poor white
neighborhood. In fact she ran their house. She told everybody what to do and what not to, including the man of the
house—he owned a service station that was losing more
money than it was making—and everybody in that household
listened. She commanded a ton of respect, so much so that
when she died in 1952, not a member of that family missed
the funeral. Often I would visit the house with my grandmother. The service station owner had a son about my age
and sometimes we would play together the whole day. If we'd
get ourselves into any sort of trouble, my grandmother would
give both of us alike her what-for. Also, if she'd give the two
of us some chore, like it or not, he'd do it, although he might
first look to his father for some signal that he could disobey
—same way that I would do to mine—but his father would
just look away. I enjoyed those days we spent together in his
house. Then we reached the age when black kids and white
kids no longer associated with each other. Society, it seemed,
forbade it; it was something that happened before you actually realized it, something you felt. Only when you got older
did you know why.

Of course, once we started school we never saw white kids
day to day. That our schools were segregated never entered
our minds. Nor did it bother us. It seemed natural, normal;
the white kids went to their school and we went to ours. They
were corn and we were rutabagas. I first went to school at
Easter Graded in the black community of Saratoga. The
large, white frame building housed four classrooms, two on
either side of the principal's office, and it was heated by a big
potbelly stove. When the weather turned cold, each morning
two or three of the older kids—the school went up to the fifth

grade—would get up early and trudge off to Easter Graded to build a fire in that big potbelly stove; it was their chore. To have the heat jumping in that big iron belly by nine, you'd have to get up as early as five o'clock in the cold and dark, but you took your turn, you shared the chore. Lessons like that never caused me any harm.

When the school term ended, I would sometimes spend the whole summer, often into harvest time, out in Windsor, Virginia, with my Aunt Martha and her sixteen children. They worked as sharecroppers on a white man's farm. Like many freed plantation slaves before them, they had no choice but to hire themselves out as tenant farmers to white landowners in order to survive after the federal government reneged on its promise to provide each black family with forty acres and a mule. For what did the freed blacks know but working the land? For their white masters they had seeded the earth and tended the crops and harvested the peanuts, tobacco, and corn, the indigo, hemp, alfalfa, and cotton. So sharecropping had become the norm in the South. When I was seven, though, I wasn't so much seeing injustices as I was enjoying the company of my cousins. We had our fun, of course, but I liked working with them, too, out in the open fields under a summer's sky. I especially remember the sky. In rural Virginia in the thirties and forties the only light we had at night came from the moon and the stars and out on the farm the night sky seemed to lie so close to the earth that I'd think you could just reach right up and with your fingers rake the firmament.

In town I lived with my mother and grandmother. My father lived just down the street. Although he and my mother deeply respected each other always, they never actually married, as my mother felt he was too old for her. He was maybe twenty-six when I was born; my mother was sixteen. All her life she lived with my grandmother, Sarah, except for one year, when I was eight or nine, that she spent in New York. She stayed with a cousin there—in the early forties, the war

years, it seemed that everybody down in Suffolk had a
cousin or some relative in New York—but after one year she
came back. She had worked in a factory packing gefilte fish.
Cooped up for long hours in a stifling gefilte fish factory
where the workers were not even allowed to speak to one
another, my mother, a young woman with a free spirit from a
small southern town of friendly, outgoing people who'd think
nothing of hollering their greetings from one side of the street
to the other, found the conditions unbearable. One thing she
said I'll never forget. She was talking to my grandmother,
and she told her that for so long as she lived she would never
ever again work for a white man.

And she never again did. My mother was strong; she inspired me. She went to Apex Beauty School to learn how to
treat and style black women's hair. She bought chemistry
books, which she studied diligently, and she began making
her own hair creams and beauty aids. I used to watch her at
her work in the kitchen with oils and powders and scents and
gelatin. I'd watch her as she'd combine her mysterious ingre-
dients, worry them, and it seemed to me magic the way they
would begin to congeal, become viscous and then thick, like
Vaseline. Her beauty treatments made her famous among
black women in the county. Even today you could go to the
south of Virginia and ask any of the older women there about
Mary Goodman, and they would tell you that woman could
do some hair.

Like my mother, I, too, went to New York for a year. In
1947. I was fourteen then, and I had started feeling that I'd
outgrown Suffolk. Night and day I dreamed of living in New
York with my uncle. I could think of nothing else I could ever
want more—until I got there. I just couldn't get used to city
ways. I'd stroll down miles of sidewalks and not one in hundreds of people would inquire how you doin', or I'd say hi
and get nothing back. For a boy coming from down south
that was strange. So I came back to Suffolk and I finished
the ninth grade, and more and more I got discouraged, irri-

table, discontented. I had left New York and had no desire at that point to return, but New York had nevertheless begun to work its way into my destiny.

I discovered myself missing simple things. We had oil lamps in Suffolk, but in New York I had been able to press a switch and see a light bulb turn on. Until I went to New York I hadn't seen a bathtub. In Suffolk a bath meant you had to first pump up water from the well and build a fire on the stove, then wait the time it took, and it took some time, to get enough water hot to fill your washtub—which is why in Suffolk you had a bath only once a week, on Saturday, so you'd be all fresh and clean for Sunday school. Waiting for my bathwater to heat, I might remember those hot- and cold-water taps in the bathrooms in New York, as well as other modern conveniences today we take for granted, and then I might also recall the big-city movie theaters and the tall buildings, the neon lights and busy streets, all the people, the constant activity. New York was a world far from this little country town in the south of Virginia. New York had made me want more than Suffolk ever dreamed of offering.

About the same time, too, I got disgusted with school. It seemed to me that I had gotten beyond my studies. I itched for adventure. I wanted to be somewhere else, somewhere totally new. Maybe I wanted to reinvent myself. I came up with a plan. My mother threw a fit.

1949

From the beginning Mary Goodman opposed the plan, and she tried to reason with her only son. He argued, he pleaded, he sulked. He begged her to sign. She refused. He persisted. For years he had dreamed of adventures in the sky like those in the war movies he never missed and comic books he devoured. In his imagination he had already worn the United States Air Force uniform, the perfectly creased trousers as blue as the sky and the long split-tail jacket with patch pockets and silver buttons. But he had dreamed long enough. That summer he turned seventeen he was ready for adventures of his own. He wanted to travel; he wanted to fly. He was underage, however, and needed his mother's signature. The more she protested the more obdurate he became. He would have his way. Protesting, Mary Goodman signed. Within days Suffolk, Virginia, had become history. Pvt. Benjamin Goodman had begun his basic USAF training at Flackman Air Force Base in San Antonio, Texas.

Six years earlier, in June 1943, Malcolm K. Little had registered at New York City's Selective Service Local Board 59; he was eighteen. At an induction center the following October the examining doctor had found him mentally disqualified for military service—the record noted a "psychopathic personality" and "sexual perversion," according to the FBI file—and he was classified 4F in December.

Since 1941 Malcolm had been working the streets of Boston and New York. His restlessness, a lack of direction, and dissatisfaction with paltry wages and dead-end jobs had taken him from shoe-shining to dishwashing to soda-jerking to waiting tables. He had also worked intermittently for the New Haven Railroad. The criminal underworld, he discovered, offered more. In New York, first under the street name of Detroit Red and later as Big Red, Malcolm began pushing dope, playing the numbers, peddling bootleg whiskey, and hustling. By 1944, still in his teens, he was often pulling in as much as two thousand dollars a month. Then, during the 1945 Christmas season in Boston, Malcolm embarked on a stealing spree that led eventually to his arrest in a second-hand jewelry store. Malcolm had left an expensive, readily identifiable, diamond-studded wristwatch, which he had stolen, with the jeweler for repair. On January 12, 1946, when he returned to reclaim the hot merchandise, a Boston police detective was waiting for him. The next month he was sentenced to a Massachusetts state prison term of eight to ten years.

In the maximum security prison at Concord Malcolm became acquainted with a fellow inmate, a Muslim brother from the Detroit temple, who brought to him the message of the Honorable Elijah Muhammad. The leader of the Nation of Islam, Malcolm learned, extolled the superiority of blacks and placed the onus for their impoverishment, joblessness, and spiritual destitution on society, a society now being ruled and corrupted by whites but soon to be destroyed by the will of Allah. The message appealed to Malcolm. In 1948 he converted to the teachings of Elijah Muhammad and embraced the promise of the new world order envisioned nearly two decades earlier by a man named Fard.

By 1949 the light Malcolm had found in Elijah Muhammad's Islamic doctrine was guiding his life. It gave purpose and direction to the desultory self-education he had begun when he first entered prison. From *aardvark* to *zymurgy* Malcolm systematically studied the dictionary. He hoarded facts; he craved knowledge. He was reading in his prison cell day and night—at night by the light of a dim bulb in the shadowy prison corridor. He was participating actively in the prison library's debating program. Indeed, the library at Norfolk Prison Colony was providing Malcolm with the training he would need for his NOI ministry. Malcolm had made of prison a seminary.

From Taejon to Tachikawa

"I have always been a Communist," stated Malcolm Little in a letter written from Charlestown State Prison on June 29, 1950, four days after the United States entered South Korea to combat the communist forces of the North. In the same letter Malcolm also claimed that during World War II he had attempted to enlist in the Japanese army—the Japanese were, after all, as Malcolm would often later point out, fighting the white oppressor of the American blacks—and had thus ensured that he'd never be drafted into the army of the United States.

Elijah Muhammad, too, had resisted the draft. When America entered World War II, he refused outright to register with the Selective Service; as a result, he was sentenced to four years in federal prison. It was also alleged that the leader of the Nation of Islam had encouraged his followers to support a Japanese victory in the Pacific because, according to Muhammad, the black Muslims and the Japanese were ethnic brothers.

Similar anti-American attitudes prevailed in the Nation of Islam during the Korean conflict. Pledging allegiance only to Allah, black Muslims refused on religious grounds to register for the draft or to serve in the armed forces. Not only did they disavow allegiance to America, but the black Muslims also forecast a moral and military defeat for America in Korea, which, they believed, would prelude the fulfillment of Islamic prophecy. They exulted; ultimately war and confla-

29

gration would spread to the shores of North America, where the black Nation of Islam, led by Allah, would rise and triumph.

Their war was not Benjamin Goodman's war, not then. In June 1950 black Muslim anti-American war propaganda would have aroused only his antipathy. When the first American troops landed in Korea on June 25, Goodman was proudly serving his country in occupied Japan, at the American air force base in Niigata. Proudly, too, he wore his USAF uniform and walked with the stride of a patriot. On sight he saluted the American flag; "The Star-Spangled Banner" and "America the Beautiful" stirred his soul.

On July 14, 1950, radar operator PFC Benjamin Goodman flew from Ashiyu Air Force Base on the Japanese island of Kyushu to Pusan, Korea, with a squadron attached to the Fifth Air Force Division under the Far East Command. It was his eighteenth birthday. He had dreamed of adventure and imagined the glories of war in the sky. He was soon to discover a new meaning for hell.

* * *

Korea's entire southern peninsula had become a battleground, *Benjamin Karim recalls,* by the time we landed in Pusan, just nineteen days after the outbreak of war. Almost immediately we were shipped north to the radar tracking sites in the mountains near Taejon. At our posts and in remote villages high in the mountains I had my first real taste of hell. I also learned that you can become accustomed to just about anything, even to hell, but you never forget those first raw shocks to your soul.

I remember seeing undernourished little kids, no more than skin on bones, scavenging in garbage cans. The war had orphaned them. Their parents may have died trying to protect them, and they had probably seen their villages as well as their homes destroyed. Reduced to no more than their wits, many of them not even close to their teens, in rags these children roamed the unfriendly mountainside and strove to keep themselves alive. In eighteen years I had never gone hungry, not one single day, and I couldn't conceive of anything so pitiable as these mountain kids wanting food that badly they had to scrounge in G.I. trash for a scrap of our leavings to eat.

I remember watching a cemetery grow. I watched as the ground got cleared until that mountainside tract looked ready for spring tillage. I remember the first body being buried in the freshly turned earth. I remember the first cross. It stood white and solitary in the new burial field, but not for long. In a week so many crosses had been planted in the land that you couldn't begin to count them.

You become accustomed to death. In a combat zone it's always there. Sometimes you think you can feel it breathing down your neck and it names your fear, but most days it's just something you escape. I particularly remember one night that I had been scheduled for patrol duty with a lieutenant in a radio jeep but at the last minute I had been replaced by another airman. We never saw him or the lieutenant again. Eventually we found the jeep. It was totally riddled with fifty-caliber bullet holes. In fact, you could not have found enough space on the body of that jeep to lay down a single silver dollar.

We often rode close to death. During the evacuation of Taejon a friend of mine, Hubert, and I somehow, in the confusion, missed our convoy back to Pusan. Luckily we spotted a supply truck traveling the same road. We flagged it down and hitched a ride in the back, on top of the truck's consignment. As we were riding along the bumpy dirt road Hubert wondered out loud, "What the hell do you think we're sitting on anyway?" I said it was probably just tinned food or something, but our curiosity was roused. So Hubert pulls out his cigarette lighter and flicks it on, and we discover we're sitting on top of a whole truckload of phosphorous

hand grenades. Had that supply truck been spotted by the
enemy, and hit, no one would have needed even to think
about looking for our dog tags. We didn't dwell on it. We had
a smoke, then lay back and went to sleep. We woke up in
Pusan. It was almost comical. As I said, in a war you become
accustomed to just about anything.

It's the deaths you don't expect that you can't accept.

Just before the evacuation of Taejon I had been informed
by a Red Cross telegram that my mother had been taken ill
and was being hospitalized for about ten days. Because her
condition was not deemed critical, my request for a stateside
leave was denied by my commanding officer. By that time I
had accumulated more than half of a good-size basketful of
Korean won in card games—my correspondence course in
cardsharping from the K.C. Card Company in Chicago had
been paying off—and I had immediately converted it, at six
hundred won to the dollar, into American currency, which I
had sent home to Suffolk. Since then I'd had no further
news. When we got back to Pusan, I began experiencing
some pretty unnerving premonitions of my mother's death,
like the foreboding I felt that sundown up in the darkening
Korean hills. I remember I was sitting on the latrine. I had
laid my rifle across my knees, and I was looking out in every
direction—I always kept my eyes watchful—but my mind
was racing, wondering about my mother because I'd not had
any word of her in nearly two weeks, when, suddenly, like a
live electric wire, this message sizzles in my brain: "Your
mother's dead," it says, and I break out into a cold sweat.
The next second I hear someone half out of breath calling out
my name. Then I see an orderly running up the hill with the
Red Cross telegram that will tell me my mother is dead.

Once I'd gotten myself pulled together I rushed down the
hillside to the compound and in a lather burst into the orderly room. I requested to speak with the commanding officer. I wanted a leave, I wanted to hop the next plane back
to the States; I wanted to attend my mother's funeral. *My*

mother, my sister, Mary, I was thinking, *she was only thirty-four and I eighteen, so we had practically grown up together and I will never see her easy smile light up a sunless day again,* when I heard the C.O. saying, "It's against air force regulations for servicemen to leave a combat zone to attend a funeral. In any case, there's no aircraft on base at this time to connect you to a stateside flight." *And I will never see my mother again.*

On one point the C.O. had lied, as I learned from one of the orderlies. That same night an airman on our base—a white man—had been granted permission to leave Pusan, and in fact had left for the States, because his wife was having a baby. Hearing that, I went cold with rage, a rage that filled the emptiness my mother's death had left inside me. It was directed at one man—the white commanding officer whose racism, and not air force regulations, I was convinced, had denied me my leave—but it also included every other white officer, new recruit, or regular serviceman whose racist assumptions had offended me. It included, too, the white owner of the gefilte fish factory in New York and any other white man who had misused my mother, like the skirt chaser who had accosted her one summer night on a quiet street in Suffolk two years before. . . .

My mother had looked like a ghost of herself that summer night, she was that shaken and drawn and out of breath. She told my grandmother how this white man had been cruising our neighborhood, how in his big car he had started following her and talking dirty to her. She cried, and a fury rose inside me. I got my gun, a .32 Colt automatic pistol my uncle had given me, and went out looking for a white man in a big car.

A white man in a big car is not difficult to find in a black neighborhood, especially if you figure he might be hankering for some of Little Charley's special corn liquor. And there he was, sitting in his big car in front of Little Charley's house. With the .32 Colt stuck in my back pocket I approached him and said, "Hey, mister, you still want that black girl you were trying so hard to get?"

"Yeah, boy," he replied, "and I'll give you a quarter if you can git her fer me."

The next thing he knew I had opened the door on the passenger side and had grabbed him at the throat with one hand while with the other I reached for my pistol. Only my cousin Jim, who had been sitting with my cousin Leon on the steps to Little Charley's house, beat me to it. He snatched the .32 from my back pocket and tossed it to Leon to keep me from using it. I kicked Jim away from me. With my fist I struck the white man hard enough to daze him. Then I un-screwed the cap on his pint of whiskey. I poured Little Char-ley's best corn liquor all over the white man's clothes and splashed what was left on the front seat of his big car. I was searching frantically in the glove compartment for a book of matches at the same time I was grappling with my cousins Jim and Leon. Together they finally managed to drag me away from the white man, his car, and my intention to set them both afire.

I was sixteen then, a minor, but had I succeeded I'd have paid. Nor would I have been the first black buck to be found hanging by his neck from a lonely tree, and who knows what other violence against our community—lynchings, rape, cas-tration—might have been committed by white men, men who need not fear the white arm of the law, in retaliation for my deed. I'd begun to become aware of the racist premises of that quiet, southern small-town world in which I was liv-ing. . . .

In Taejon I had picked up a Chinese burp gun—a short-barreled, fully automatic submachine gun with a cylindrical spring-loaded magazine that holds ninety rounds of ammuni-tion. I sat on my footlocker in my tent on the compound at Pusan and round by round I loaded the burp gun's maga-zine. Round by round I thought about the white man in the big car and all the others like him—all of them "worse than the devil," my mother would say, but "for their wickedness God will pay them back," she would say. Round by round I remembered sneers, insults, gibes, threats; too long I had tolerated, as every black man had, the injustices of white supremacists, civilians and military men alike. Round by round every racist one of them in my mind at that moment converged in my commanding officer. I locked the magazine into its housing. Without fear and with ninety rounds of ammunition I walked out of my tent and across the compound toward the orderly room. I was not going to wait for God.

I never made it to the C.O.'s office. Outside my tent I met a buddy who detoured me. He talked me out of my plan and he may have talked some sense into me, but he didn't talk me out of my anger.

Not long after that I was shipped back to Japan. I spent the next two years first at Niigata Air Force Base on the Sea of Japan and then at Tachikawa Air Force Base near Tokyo. At Tachikawa I awoke every morning to a view of the distant, snow-capped peak of Mt. Fujiyama in the window above my bed, and every day held for me the experience of freedom, which raised my spirits even more. Japan redefined for me the meaning of freedom. For the first time, it seemed, freedom was more than a word. No signs announced WHITES IN FRONT, COLOREDS IN THE REAR, and public toilets did not accommodate "whites only" or "coloreds only." At shop counters you didn't have to stand in a designated niche and wait however long it was going to take the white clerk to decide to ask you, with contempt, "Watcha wan', nigra?" Nor did arrogant teenage white boys walk together shoulder to shoulder down the sidewalk and force you off the curb into the gutter. You heard no heart-sickening stories of black men being lynched or castrated for some supposed effrontery to a white woman or of black girls being raped for a white man's pleasures.

You did, however, have to deal with the propaganda and lies of white servicemen. I remember one occasion when another black airman and I were approached by two Japanese women who wanted to rub our skin. They seemed quite surprised when they examined their hands afterward. "You no painted," they said. "White G.I. lie." More invidious were rumors that we carried deadly diseases, that we would rape their women, that we kidnapped children and ate them alive. Too, some white servicemen, officers among them, threatened to take their business elsewhere if Japanese proprietors continued to serve blacks in their establishments. (The Japanese always apologized to us for the inconvenience.) White Americans, it appeared, did not hesitate to transplant their racial hatred in foreign soil. Furthermore, at no time during my two-year tour of duty at Tachikawa Air Force Base did any white officer, NCO, or G.I. ever speak to this issue. Discrimination was clearly if not officially sanctioned by the military in the early 1950s.

The anger that had erupted so violently inside me that night in Pusan when my white C.O. refused me permission to attend my mother's funeral evolved in Japan into an intense resentment of white authority in America's racially biased military system. That system had denied me a promotion in Pusan. At Tachikawa in Japan, where I again earned a reputation among the airmen as the best radar operator and radio monitor on the base, I again was not promoted beyond my rank of private first class by the white commanding officers. My case was not, of course, the exception among African Americans in the armed forces. I nevertheless developed an attitude problem.

I remember traveling across Japan by train. Outside the window endless rice paddies, forests of pine and cedar and bamboo, pagodas, clusters of trim wood houses, all sped familiarly by. It seemed as if I'd known this landscape my entire lifetime, and when I looked around the coach, I found a kinship in the faces of the Japanese passengers. I felt a profound affinity with these people and their land. Then I considered the faces of the white American military men around me, men who for the most part regarded not only me and all African Americans but also the Japanese with repugnance and racist disdain, and I was sickened by them. My countrymen had become strangers to me, aliens. I decided I wanted never to live in the United States again.

When my tour of duty with the USAF was nearing its end, I submitted my official request to be discharged in Japan. That request was denied. I was assigned to Kirkland Air Force Base in Albuquerque, New Mexico.

Before reporting for duty at Kirkland, I went home to Suffolk on leave for a few days. In two years, in my despondency over my mother's death, I had written to no one, not even my grandmother. So she was surprised when I walked into her house with my duffel bag. And shocked. She threw her arms up over her head and started screaming at the top of her voice. "My baby, my baby," she cried again and again. "My baby," she finally managed to blubber, "they told us you were dead."

I then discovered the circumstances of my mother's death. By telegram she had received official notification from the government that her son, PFC Benjamin Goodman, serial number 13319507, had been killed in action. Ten days later she herself was dead. That telegram had killed her. She had tried to dull the pain and grief over her only child's death with a bottle of corn liquor. She had been smoking a cigarette; she'd fallen asleep. The mattress had caught fire. Mostly there was just a lot of smoke, but my mother had gotten burned—not so seriously burned, though, as to do her near mortal harm. Still, she hadn't recovered. In the hospital—the inadequate black hospital eighty miles away in Richmond—she had not responded to anything, not to any medication, not to any treatment. She didn't want to live because I was dead. She had told everybody that. Everybody said that "Mary could have just up and walked right out of there, but she wouldn't take to any doctor's medicine,

Dickie-boy, or to anybody's caring, for she was grieving so bad, and she just died.''

The military had made a dreadful mistake. Some poor dead serviceman's dog tag had been incorrectly read and in error the government had sent a telegram to the mother of Benjamin Goodman. So everybody had thought that I was dead, except for the Red Cross. A few days later they were sending me a telegram about my mother's ill health and hospitalization, and who knows where the money I'd won at cardsharping and sent from Pusan had landed. An image settled in my mind: a rigid jaw and curled lip, a nose like an eagle's beak, and then the hard, unsympathetic blue-eyed gaze of the white C.O. who had denied me my last chance both to see my young mother alive and to honor her dead. It reignited the murderous anger I'd felt two years earlier in Pusan; it enlarged every resentment since. It scorched my soul. I didn't know it then, but I was already ready for Malcolm X.

1952–1956

In September 1952, at Kirkland Air Force Base in Albuquerque, New Mexico, PFC Benjamin Goodman received a general discharge under honorable conditions from the United States Air Force. For three years he had served in arms a country he had learned to abhor. Like many African Americans who had been stationed in occupied Japan during the Korean War, he had experienced personal freedom daily, vitally, and each day had pointed up to him the cruel hypocrisy of human liberty in his native land. Embittered by white America's racism, the young veteran dreamed of returning to Japan. Dreams, though, could not lessen the distance westward in miles and ocean from Albuquerque to Niigata. To the east lay sleepy Suffolk. It offered neither an alternative nor solace, for in the small town's graveyard for coloreds both Mary and Sarah, his mother and grandmother, now lay dead. His mother's brother Walter Lee, he had heard, was making a decent living for himself up north, in New York. He decided eventually to give the unfriendly city of neon another try.

That same September, in Detroit, a parolee from the Massachusetts state prison system was officially named Malcolm X by the Nation of Islam. On that occasion Malcolm K. Little forever renounced the slave name that for generations had yoked his paternal forebears to white oppression. "X stands for the unknown," Malcolm said in a 1963 WUST radio interview—unknown because the true family names of black

41

Americans, their African family names, had been obliterated
four hundred years before by their white slavemasters.

Malcolm K. Little had been released from prison on August 7, 1952. On August 8 he had traveled by bus from Boston to Detroit, where his brother Wilfred, the head of a
Muslim household and manager of a furniture store in the
city's black ghetto, had offered him a job and a home. He
also introduced Malcolm to Detroit Temple Number One.
The temple, as it happened, was sponsoring a motor caravan
to the NOI headquarters in Chicago on Labor Day weekend.
The brothers and sisters from Detroit would be attending
Sunday services conducted by the Messenger Elijah Muhammad himself. Malcolm's anticipation was keen, his expectations high. He was not disappointed. As Malcolm recounts it
in the *Autobiography*, "it was like an electrical shock"
when, at the end of the service, Elijah Muhammad singled
Malcolm out and praised him for the faith and strength he
had demonstrated in prison. That evening Elijah Muhammad entertained Malcolm in his home. Malcolm would share
many more dinners with Elijah Muhammad and his gentle
wife, Sister Clara, at their house in Chicago over the next
two years, for that evening Malcolm had found in Elijah
Muhammad a personal mentor and in Malcolm Elijah
Muhammad had found his spiritual son.

The next day Malcolm returned to Detroit. At the time he
was working as a salesman with his brother at the furniture
store. In January 1953 he joined the assembly line first at
Ford's Lincoln-Mercury division (for one week) and then at
Gar Wood, a manufacturer of bodies for garbage trucks. In
every case Malcolm found the work mindless, the boredom
oppressive. Daily his spirits flagged. Malcolm wanted a mission.

Benjamin Goodman wanted a job, when he arrived in New
York late in November 1952, that would put his military
training to civilian use. His background in radar operations,
however, failed to secure him a position in the control tower

at either La Guardia Airport or Idlewild. He then applied for admission into New York's police academy, and was rejected; he was underweight. After working for a time with his uncle, who was prospering as a house painter, he took a less demanding job with a clothing manufacturer in the Garment District. To supplement his meager income he started gambling. Often all night he sat in on neighborhood poker games in Harlem, and he was soon raking in enough money to quit his daytime job and get some sleep. Eventually, though, he played himself out of the poker-game circuit in Harlem. His cardsharper's winning streak had become dangerously suspect.

In June 1953 Malcolm X was named the assistant minister at Temple Number One. He was soon dedicating all his energies and time to forwarding the black Muslim movement in Detroit. He permanently left the blue-collar workplace and went "fishing," as he called it. He began canvassing the streets of the black ghetto—the very streets a man named Fard had worked twenty years before—and to the underprivileged and underpaid he brought Fard's message of imminent salvation for the lost who were found in the Nation of Islam. Elijah Muhammad wanted converts, recruits, members, dues. He had asked Detroit for thousands. Malcolm strove to deliver.

The following December the Messenger dispatched the missionary to Boston. Like Fard at his Islamic house meetings in 1930, Malcolm spoke to a small group of Muslims in a ghetto living room. The group soon outgrew the room. By March 1954 Malcolm had recruited enough converts to open Boston Temple Number Eleven. He moved on to Philadelphia. Dissension within the Muslim brotherhood there had long been crippling its effectiveness and diminishing its membership. In three months, as the acting minister, Malcolm had restored order and established sound NOI control at Philadelphia Temple Number Twelve. Before the end of 1954 Malcolm would repeat such successes with the establishment of Tem-

ple Number Thirteen in Springfield, Massachusetts, and
Temple Number Fourteen in Hartford. By that time, too, he
was back on the streets of Harlem, hustling.

Storefront quarters in a derelict Harlem neighborhood
housed the Nation of Islam in New York when Malcolm was
appointed minister of Temple Number Seven in June 1954.
Its membership was scant, its name barely known, its voice
small and unheard in the din of Harlem's street-corner discontent. Malcolm knew Harlem's streets and he knew how to
hustle, only now he wasn't dealing dope or whores. He was
selling Islam. He distributed leaflets. He went "fishing" on
the street corners where ardent black nationalists shouted
their slogans and gathered their crowds. He raided the black
Christian churches and proselytized. Success came only in
degrees. Slowly his congregation grew, too slowly for Malcolm. It was already 1956. He needed publicity, he needed
exposure; he needed an event, a rallying cry, a cause.

In the fall of 1956, when Benjamin Goodman was working
in the shipping room at Vanguard Records, he met a black
Muslim named Brother Leo. Brother Leo spoke often of "the
Minister," and each week he pressed Goodman to accom-
pany him to a class "the Minister" was teaching at the Muslim temple. The class was titled The Black Man's History.
Goodman scoffed. In his view, at that time, the black man
had no history worth studying. He imagined native Africans
the way he remembered them from illustrated schoolbooks,
magazines, comic books, and movies: as half-naked savages
stalking through tropical jungle, as bearers for great white
hunters on safari, as some curious subspecies that communi-
cated in silver-screen gibberish, as cannibals. He resisted
Brother Leo's weekly invitations. Neither the history nor the
temple nor "the Minister" interested him.

What happened in Harlem one Sunday evening the following spring changed all that.

Harlem, April 1957

It was not uncommon. In the 1950s white police officers were constantly, and often brutally, harassing blacks on the Harlem sidewalks; the offense could as easily be loitering as assault or robbery. So Hinton Johnson, a Muslim brother at Temple Number Seven, was probably not particularly surprised by what he saw on a Harlem street corner that Sunday evening in April 1957. But he was outraged. "You're not in Alabama! This is New York," he cried at the two white policemen who were billy-whipping a black man they had apprehended. The officers ordered Johnson to move on. He refused. They responded with their nightsticks. After clubbing him down to the ground, they began striking him repeatedly on the side of the head. Then they placed Johnson under arrest.

Word of the incident quickly reached the minister at Temple Number Seven, and within the half hour Malcolm had led a contingent of Muslim brothers to the 28th Precinct on 123rd Street. Inside the police station Malcolm demanded that he be allowed to see and personally verify Johnson's condition. The police refused to comply. Meanwhile, outside the station, behind Malcolm's well-disciplined Muslims was gathering an unruly crowd of young Harlemites, curious bystanders, church people, store owners, housewives, mothers, children. Many of them had never before heard of Malcolm X; some were armed. Policemen were isolated from each other in tight pockets inside the angry crowd. Any minute protest might erupt into violence.

Only one person could disperse the crowd and avert a riot, newspaper editor James Hicks advised the deputy police commissioner. That person was Malcolm X. Malcolm met with the commissioner and two police inspectors in Hicks's office at the *Amsterdam News*. Malcolm would disband the demonstrators, he said, on the condition that he be permitted to see for himself that Johnson was receiving proper medical attention. The commissioner agreed.

The police brutality had in fact left Hinton Johnson barely conscious. Malcolm managed to contain his rage, and a police ambulance rushed Johnson from the station house to Sydenham Hospital where a neurosurgeon attended to him immediately. Hundreds of blacks from all over Harlem spilled into the streets outside Sydenham.

Once Malcolm had been assured by the police that Johnson would continue to receive medical treatment and that his assailants would be punished, Malcolm stepped outside the station. His orderly contingent of Muslims and the restive crowd behind them awaited him. They numbered well over two thousand. In silence Malcolm stood before them. "And then," as James Hicks describes the moment in Peter Goldman's *The Death and Life of Malcolm X*, "in that dim light, Malcolm stood up and waved his hand, and all those people just disappeared. *Disappeared*. One of the police people said to me, 'Did you see what I just saw?' I said, 'Yeah.' He said, 'This is too much power for one man to have.' He meant one black man."

Harlem had found a champion.

* * *

That Sunday—April 14, 1957—changed it all, *Benjamin Karim recalls*, for Malcolm, for Harlem, for me. When that white police officer struck down Hinton Johnson and beat him near to death for talking back, he also struck a nerve in the black community. For a long time the nerve had been sore, only this time we were not too numb to know it. Because of a man called Malcolm X. Because of him thousands of blacks from all over Harlem banded together—at the police station, at the hospital, at last—to protest.

By the next morning everyone in Harlem had heard of Malcolm X and his black Muslims. All day, no matter where you went, people were talking of nothing else. A black man had challenged white authority; he had stood up to the entire police force at the 28th Precinct, including the deputy police commissioner, and he'd gotten away with it. I knew no one then who would even have dreamed of striding into a police station full of white officers and demanding that a victim of white police brutality, a black man, be moved to a hospital for proper treatment, and yet this man named X had done just that. It was a first.

For the first time, too, the general public had had the opportunity to observe the Fruit of Islam, the Muslim brothers from Temple Number Seven, in action. All those people outside the 123rd Street station had been impressed by the brothers' clean-cut appearance—their hair cut close to the head and their faces clean shaven, they wore dark suits with fresh white shirts and conservative ties—and their proud, soldierly bearing. The brothers had stood fearlessly in the face of an armed, mostly white police force. Like a well-drilled military unit, like an extension of the body of their leader, they had responded to the unspoken commands of the minister of Temple Number Seven; meticulous training had made instinct of their discipline. The more I heard about the whole episode the more I wanted to be one of those men. I resolved to attend the services at the temple the next Sunday.

I was amazed. By the hundreds, it seemed, people were arriving at the storefront temple on the corner of 116th Street and Lenox Avenue, which has since been renamed Malcolm X Boulevard. Fortunately I had planned to get there early, so I was among the first to be admitted into the temple that Sunday afternoon.

At the 116th Street entrance two conservatively dressed young men politely greeted me with a "Welcome, brother," and I entered the hallway where two more well-groomed Muslims directed me up a single flight of stairs. At the top of the stairs the woman ahead of me was directed to the right. I was asked to proceed to my left, into the men's room. Just inside the door a brother pointed me toward one of four other men who were standing bolt upright in front of a long table. A stocky man over six feet tall—he was about my height—leaned toward me until his face was less than twelve inches from mine. Firmly but not threateningly he asked, "Do you have any weapons, alcohol, cigarettes, or drugs in your possession?" I replied that I didn't, and realized that he was leaning so close to me in order to determine if I had alcohol on my breath. If he had, I would have been requested to leave. I was next instructed to remove the contents of my pockets and place them on the table. Had I been carrying a weapon, a half pint, or cigarettes, which were prohibited inside the temple, they would have been withheld from me until the service was over. "I would now like to check your person, please," he said, and asked me to raise my arms. With one of his feet planted firmly between the two of mine he ran his hands down the sleeves of my suit jacket. Then, his hands inside my jacket, he ran them up my back. He thrust his thumbs inside the waistband of my trousers on either side of my spine and brought them around to the clasp on my fly. He asked me to spread my legs. He placed one hand on my left thigh and the other at my crotch. He ran his hands down the length of my left leg to the cuff of my trousers. He did the same with the right. Then he pressed against the leather uppers of my shoes. He asked me to turn around and raise my foot back toward him. He inspected the left heel to be certain it was nailed secure. He checked the heel of the right. Last of all he aimed my ballpoint pen at me. He clicked the push button twice. Satisfied, he returned my belongings and thanked me for my cooperation. He told me I could proceed to the auditorium.

A young man in a dark suit and tie waited at the open double doors to the auditorium. On the far wall, at the opposite end of the center aisle, hung the portrait of a small-boned, serene-looking man. A crescent moon and stars shone on the crown of his brimless hat, and his luminous eyes seemed to follow me as I was ushered down the aisle and seated in the order of my arrival near the front of the auditorium. I resisted the urge to turn around and gawk. Perhaps I had been expecting an atmosphere more like that of a circus. Certainly I had not expected the formality. Cordial but alert, the brothers and sisters in charge had the situation entirely under control, and nothing or no one escaped their scrutiny. At the same time, though, even when they were searching you —which was necessary—they made you feel totally welcome and comfortable, like a special guest in their home. I felt sheltered. I felt immediately that this was the place I wanted to be, needed to be, that here I could grow. And for the next seven years I would. I would grow spiritually and intellectually. I would pursue knowledge, exercise my mind, enlarge my capabilities; I would learn.

In fact, I had already started. A blackboard on the platform at the front of the auditorium had taken my attention. On either side of the blackboard had been painted a cross and a crescent. On one side, too, was an American flag with each of four words in capital letters—CHRISTIANITY, SLAVERY, SUFFERING, DEATH—at each of its four corners. Opposite it, at each corner of a red flag emblazoned with a crescent moon and a star, had been printed ISLAM, FREEDOM, JUSTICE, EQUALITY. Between the two flags had been written the question "Who will survive the War of Armageddon?" I had heard of Armageddon in Sunday school when I was growing up. It was Christian teaching; in the final cosmic battle between the forces of good and of evil the devil would be forever destroyed and the supremacy of God would be established on earth. The picture beneath the question on the blackboard, however, had roused my thoughts more. It showed a black man hanging from a tree by a rope around his neck. As a child in southern Virginia I had grown up with stories of lynchings, and I might have even faced one myself had I lit that white man in the big car nine years before, but this picture in the middle of the display on the blackboard was really disturbing me.

At that point one of the assistant ministers stepped up to the platform. "*Assalaam alaikum,*" he said, and then translated the traditional Arabic greeting: "Peace be unto you." He introduced himself as Brother Henry. Turning our attention to the American flag on the blackboard, he began by explaining the significance of the four words at its corners. The white man in America, he said, had twisted the interpretation of the Bible to suit his own evil purpose, which was to imprison the black man in a white man's religion, in CHRISTIANITY. The white man had convinced our forebears that his white God had willed us into SLAVERY. He had taught them that they were the descendants of Ham, whose line was cursed by his father, Noah; because Ham had looked upon his father when he lay drunk and naked in his bed, Noah condemned Canaan, the innocent son of the disrespectful Ham, to a lifetime of servitude. For the sins of Ham, supposedly, blacks in America had been destined by God to submit to the whims of their supposed superiors, the white Christian slavemasters. For four hundred years suppositions like these had ensured black people's SUFFERING. For four hundred years Christianity had spelled DEATH for them. All the black people who were transported to America on slave ships, Brother Henry reminded us, were not born Christian. In Africa they had had their own religion, and their own language, culture, history, traditions, but they had been uprooted from their native land, and in America the white oppressor had used holy scripture to justify both the loss of their freedom and the death of their African heritage. So each new generation of blacks had been born more hopelessly into spiritual as well as economic bondage. Nor had any of them ever seen a single penny in payment for the fortunes reaped from the white man's land at the cost of a black people's labors, lifeblood, suffering, and soul.

Stating that Armageddon would alter the course of events for blacks in America, Brother Henry crossed to the other side of the blackboard. God was black and the devil white, he said. God would bring white America to its knees and destroy it in the sight of all the nations of the world, he said, and pointed to the word at the top left corner of the crescent flag: ISLAM. I learned then that *Islam* in Arabic means "submission to the will of God." From Abraham to Muhammad all the prophets had submitted to Allah, the uninterpretable name the Muslims give to God. I learned too that in Arabic *mu* means "one" and *salim* means "in submission," so all Muslims, like the prophets themselves, submit only to the will of God. And not to the whims of white authority.

I had not noticed that meanwhile another man had stepped onto the platform. He was sitting behind Brother Henry at a small table near the wall. Even sitting down he looked tall. I also thought he looked young—more like twenty-five, my age then, than thirty-two—but distinguished too, imposing. Neither his easy posture nor the dark blue suit he wore with a white shirt and red tie could camouflage the energy in his presence. An open briefcase sat beside him on the floor and on the tabletop lay two books. He seemed to be studying a handful of three-by-five index cards; occasionally he made notations. He pushed his horn-rimmed glasses back up the bridge of his nose. He looked up, as if on instinct, when the assistant minister paused to introduce him. He looked serious, but you could see a hint of a smile on his lips and his light complexion took on a glow.

The assistant minister said that Brother Minister Malcolm would give us a clearer understanding of the teachings of the Honorable Elijah Muhammad and a better understanding of ourselves. Brother Minister Malcolm gathered together the index cards and picked up the two books on the table. He rose and shook the assistant minister's hand. He took the podium.

He was tall. Malcolm stood close to six-foot-four. Though slender, his trim body spoke strength. His grayish eyes spoke intelligence. Malcolm surveyed the room a moment, and his eyes held us in a power like a spell. It seemed as if he could see right into us and any emptiness he found there he could fill with his compassion. In the ensuing months and years I would learn to read in Malcolm's eyes his many moods and emotions. I would see their soft gray shadows go hard and cold as the Arctic. I would recognize their angry fire; I'd see them dance with humor. I'd seek their warm comprehension and sympathy when some problem at the temple or at home seemed to be too much for me.

Malcolm didn't rush. He laid down the two books, one on top of the other (they were the Bible and the Koran), on the podium. He methodically sorted the index cards. Everyone in the auditorium waited. Every seat was filled, and wherever they could people were standing around the sides and in the aisles. Another thousand people waited outside the auditorium, in the corridor, all the way down the stairs to the entrance and out onto 116th Street and Lenox. *"Assalaam alaikum,"* Malcolm welcomed us, "it's good to see so many of you here at the Temple of Islam."

Malcolm leaned slightly forward on the podium. The light caught the reddish tint in his hair. "And now I'll tell you why you are here," he said. "You are here because you are

black. It doesn't matter how light or how dark your complexion is because if you're not white, you're black, and the fact
that you are here proves you're black.'' You could tell some
of the audience felt uncomfortable with that. They felt
maybe that to congregate as blacks in such large numbers
might attract the police. Malcolm sensed their discomfort. He
told them not to worry, that if the police came busting into
Temple Number Seven, their bodies would be piling up at the
door. Here and there in the auditorium you could hear
laughter, some of it muffled and nervous, some of it appreciative.

As the laughter quieted, Malcolm contemplated the books
he had placed on the podium. After a few seconds he held up
the Bible with his right hand. Pointing with his left to the
portrait on the wall behind him, he told us that the Honorable Elijah Muhammad, the Messenger of Allah, called this
book the poison book. Poison in the hands of a doctor can be
a medicine, it can cure, he said, but in the hands of a fool
poison is death. And Christian ministers, he continued, are
fools, including especially the ninety-nine-point-nine percent
of black Christian preachers who have been poisoning the
minds of their black parishioners with a white man's religion
for years. Or else they freeze the brains of black people
numb with their lessons and scriptures. Mr. Muhammad tells
us that Christian preachers are ice men, said Malcolm, and
their church is an icehouse where black people, their minds
frozen senseless, believe what they're taught. They believe
they are the children of Ham, a man cursed in his drunkenness by his father and God. Or they believe they are the
children of Hagar, the Egyptian servant girl who obeyed her
childless mistress, Sarah, and lay down with Abraham, her
master, so that she might bear him a son, only to be banished
into the desert with the boychild Ishmael that was born to
them. A white man's religion has convinced black people that
they are either cursed or outcast and born to obey and honor

their master no matter what injuries and injustices he may force them to endure.

Just as the minds of our forebears were poisoned by scripture, Malcolm told us, so were their bodies poisoned by pork. Our slave ancestors were fed, Malcolm said, on the pig's offal, on its entrails, feet, tail, ears, and testicles. And what were the pigs fed on? Slops and filth; dead rats, maggots, garbage. Sows eat the piglets they can't nurse, Malcolm told us, and if a pig falls ill and isn't removed from the pen, the other pigs will soon devour it. No wonder, then, that fluke worms and all the other parasites of swine are hosted in the pig's flesh and organs and intestines. No wonder, either, that our people were so often being taken sick, groaned Malcolm. They were eating disease every time they ate of the pig.

Malcolm lectured at length on the pig, and I began thinking about the ones that we had raised in our yard back in Suffolk. We used to collect what we called swill. We'd dump any scraps and unwanted leftovers and spoiled foods into a large metal garbage can. Then, after the supper dishes had gotten washed, we'd take the day's basin of dishwater and pour it into the can; we'd throw dead rats in there, too. We kept a lid on the garbage, but of course flies would get into it anyway, and lay their eggs, so the swill would be teeming with maggots by the time the can was full and we'd throw its contents to the pigs. Still, we'd eat their meat and find it good.

Although Malcolm discussed many subjects in the course of his lecture that day, he spoke hardly at all about the Hinton Johnson incident. He did mention the meeting arranged by the editor of the *Amsterdam News* with the deputy police commissioner. He said the police had learned that from now on when police violence comes down on a Muslim brother, or sister, they will be dealing with Malcolm X.

A question-answer period followed Malcolm's lecture. I had quite a few questions in my mind; so much of what Malcolm had said seemed to relate to my own experience with white authority, especially when I was in the military. With so many questions tumbling over each other at the same time, however, I couldn't seem to formulate even one. Malcolm himself had a few questions. He asked us to raise our hands if we believed that what he had spoken and what we had heard was true. I raised mine. He then asked those of us who had raised our hands if we were ready to join our own kind. Again I raised my hand.

I had in fact begun my adoption into the Lost-Found Nation of Islam. I was told that after I had attended two more meetings I would be given a letter regarding the Nation and my role in it. I would have to copy out this letter perfectly by hand, and it would then be sent to the national headquarters in Chicago for approval. Once it had been approved I would receive my X.

By the time I left the temple my mind was feeling like a big ball of twine unraveling inside my head. To sort out all the new ideas, concepts, and arguments that Malcolm had spoken and that I had heard would take time. One of them, though, I discovered that evening, had made a very distinct impression on me. I had been invited to dinner at the house of two old family friends in Brooklyn. They were serving some of my favorite dishes. On one side of the table sat a huge bowl of homemade potato salad, on the other a bowl of collard greens cooked with salt pork, and in the center a large platter of pigs' feet. They knew my appetite, which was a lot less slim than my size, and piled the food high on my plate. I cut off a tiny piece of meat from a pig's foot. I put it in my mouth, and suddenly I felt queasy. My face went hot, my head seemed light. I tried to ignore what I was feeling. I tried to chew the bit of meat, or swallow it, but couldn't. I could think only of fluke worms and swill. I was breaking into a sweat and any second my stomach might be betraying me. I rushed from the room. I have not eaten a single bite of pork since.

Inside the Temple

The membership at New York Temple Number Seven jumped from a few hundred to several thousand after the Hinton Johnson incident. Affiliation with the Nation of Islam required prospective Muslim brothers and sisters to copy out by hand an official letter of application in which they stated their readiness to join unto their own kind. The letter established that applicants had attended a designated number of meetings at a particular temple and that they had believed what had been spoken and what they had heard there. Only when this document had been delivered to the national headquarters in Chicago with every word perfectly spelled and every comma, apostrophe, hyphen, and colon correctly placed would the applicant under review be granted membership and awarded an X.

The process could take months. After his first meeting at Temple Number Seven on April 21, 1957, Benjamin Goodman submitted his first letter of application. Not until the following August, after several more unsuccessful attempts, did he complete the letter-perfect application that would officially gain him his brotherhood in the Nation of Islam. Up to that time Goodman had been living with a genial young woman named Cora. Because the NOI forbade extramarital relationships, he now had two choices: he could marry Cora or he could abandon her. He and Cora agreed to marry. Cora also converted to Islam. From the beginning she found the moral rigor of the black Muslim community difficult.

Eventually she found it stifling. She longed for the occasional night at a jazz club or bar; she missed parties, movies, popular music. She had an eye for stylish clothes. The marriage lasted six years. "She just got lonely for the world," says Benjamin Karim.

In January 1958 Malcolm X married Betty Sanders. She had joined the New York temple in 1956. Intelligent, capable, attractive, Sister Instructor Betty X had not escaped the notice of the brother minister, although she didn't know it. Having sought the counsel only of himself and the Honorable Elijah Muhammad, Malcolm reached his decision on the morning of January 13. From a pay phone at a gas station in Detroit Malcolm called the unsuspecting Betty at her nursing-school residence in New York, according to Bruce Perry's *Malcolm: The Life of the Man Who Changed America*. Sister Betty had barely said hello when, to her astonishment, the magnetic but aloof brother minister was proposing marriage. A civil ceremony was performed the very next day, a Tuesday, by a justice of the peace in Lansing. The following Sunday Malcolm and Betty attended services at Detroit Temple Number One, where the Honorable Elijah Muhammad's announcement of their wedding surprised the entire Nation—and very much disappointed the unwed among its sisterhood. After the service the newlyweds drove back to New York in Malcolm's new car. They took up residence in East Elmhurst, Queens, and daily, proudly, in his new dark blue Oldsmobile, Malcolm commuted to Temple Number Seven at 102 West 116th Street in Harlem.

* * *

I found a home, *asserts Benjamin Karim,* when I joined the NOI. Malcolm, his assistant ministers, the staff, Captain Joseph, the brothers, the sisterhood, they all became my family. At Number Seven we lived inside another world, a world with customs, rules, rituals, and a morality of its own. I was happy to inhabit it. It changed my life profoundly. It changed not only the way I thought but also the way I walked, dressed, drank, spoke, listened, ate. And I'm not just talking pork.

It is said that in the East the Prophet Fard had known a man who had then been living two hundred and forty years. Fard had asked the aged man the secret of his longevity. "Beans," the ancient had replied. "Beans," Fard told his people, and on the old man's secret built our Muslim diet.

Bean soups, bean salads, bean pies—in some form or other beans appear in every good Muslim's daily meal. Along with beans at the base of the Muslim diet are grains. Before I joined the brotherhood at the temple I always enjoyed sliced white bread with no thought to health or nutrients, just as I had always eaten processed white rice. Muslims, though, make their own whole-grain breads, and they eat only brown rice. They also use only raw sugar. After beans and grains, next in dietary importance come fruits of all kinds and vegetables, root vegetables and vine vegetables and any variety of leafy vegetable except for collard greens. The Muslim diet also includes meat, especially lamb—Malcolm would light into a plate of braised lamb shanks like a bear going for honey—and we'd eat halal chicken. But absolutely no pork or pork by-products. Muslims don't eat slave food, and even soaps and lipsticks that might contain the fat of the unclean pig are forbidden.

Muslims eat only one meal a day, usually in the evening after sundown, but there is more nutrition in that one Muslim meal than in the three square ones most Christian people eat. The Muslim meals I remember best I shared with Malcolm at his house in East Elmhurst. Malcolm would sometimes invite his assistant ministers—I was made an assistant minister in 1958—over to Queens for dinner after the Sunday meeting. At a Sunday service Malcolm would often speak four hours at least, so by the time we'd leave the temple it would already be after six and we assistants would be elated. These dinners were occasions. I don't know that I recall any times happier than the leisurely Sunday evenings we spent with Malcolm in his home. He was the perfect host, and Sister Betty, his wife, made sure that we didn't leave the table in any way unsatisfied.

Of course, no alcoholic drinks were served on these occasions; all alcohol was prohibited. Brother Omar, however, might have prepared his watermelon nectar, which took on the color of delicate pink tea roses, or a lime-colored ade of fresh citrus, and we'd always have a choice of ginger ale or our own homemade ginger beer, or milk. Betty and a kitchen full of Muslim sisters who justly prided themselves on their Islamic cookery would meanwhile be setting a feast on the dinner table. The sisters competed with each other for our praise, each one trying to outdo the other, and they'd present us with a tableful of savory, mouthwatering dishes, platters, and casseroles. After a bean soup seasoned with aromatic herbs and spices, which we ate with homemade whole-wheat bread, would follow eight or nine courses of hors d'oeuvres, all of them equally tempting, and then maybe a lamb roast or braised lamb shanks or barbecued chicken. We'd have a choice of sauces for the meat as well as brown rice, green vegetables, and a variety of fresh salads. All the recipes for our dishes were issued by Mr. Muhammad, who was our guide in all things, but the sisters would introduce their own delicious—and very well-kept—secrets into them. And what secrets they baked into cakes and pies! Unforgettable as the carrot cakes were, my favorite dessert was bean pie, which tasted just like sweet-potato pie, topped with a scoop of Häagen-Dazs vanilla ice cream. We all loved Häagen-Dazs ice cream. Whenever we went visiting another

Muslim household, we would take along some Häagen-Dazs for hospitality. It cost eighty-six cents a pint.

No one left Malcolm's table hungry. We'd sit down with appetites as healthy as Malcolm's—that man could eat!—but we would take care not to overeat. Overeating, Malcolm taught us, not only taxes the digestive system but also clouds the intellect and slows down mental activity. Malcolm taught us to pace ourselves at the dinner table, to savor the taste of each dish, to eat moderately, and to observe ritual. He said that you can tell a lot about a man by the way he eats, and he himself set us a meticulous example. Malcolm ate slowly, in silence, as if he were contemplating the flavor of every bite. His posture erect, his napkin in his lap, he always took the food to his mouth and never slurped, fumbled, gobbled, or blew on it. His cutlery never clanked against his plate and he wouldn't eat a salad with a meat fork. He never rested his elbows on the table. The man had style, grace. Amy Vanderbilt would have had to sweat to match him. So would a surgeon. Malcolm could work a knife and fork with such precision that he could carve meat from the breast of a chicken and leave the bones on his plate looking like they had been sucked clean without ever once touching one of them with his fingers.

Malcolm always drank a whole quart of milk with his evening meal. Betty would bring it to the table in a pitcher and pour it for him into a tall glass. On one of these occasions, I particularly remember, Betty came in from the kitchen with the milk and glass as usual, but you could tell something was ruffling her by the weighty silence that accompanied her, and her face was somber. We were between courses, so Malcolm was talking, and he continued talking without looking up at Betty when she set the glass down in front of him. You could hear its emptiness. She put the pitcher down beside it. The milk lapped toward the spout. Malcolm continued talking and Betty started to leave the room. She was about to step across the threshold into the kitchen when Malcolm, without even a glance toward her, said, "Pour it." Betty stopped dead in her tracks. She seemed to be considering some alternative. Then she walked back to the table. She picked up the pitcher. And she poured it. She poured the milk nearly to the brim of Malcolm's glass and not a drop spilled off the spout when she placed the pitcher back down on the table. Malcolm was still talking when she left the room.

After we had finished our desserts at these Sunday dinners and the sisters had served our coffee, Malcolm would open up a conversation. He might start discussing temple policy or instructing us in Islam, or he might let us air our own questions and concerns. These after-dinner sessions did not include the sisters. We never discussed matters of policy with our wives and families or friends or relatives because we did not want to burden them with information that might disturb or upset them. Some things, too, they were the better for not knowing. Sometimes we would sit talking at that table with Malcolm for hours, and we'd know him not just as our brother minister but as a counselor, a father, a wise man, a master, a friend. You felt you didn't need anyone else.

Whatever we were discussing or doing would stop at eight o'clock for one half hour. That's when the radio broadcasted the Honorable Elijah Muhammad's Sunday evening message out of Chicago. We would all listen intently, respectfully, all us brothers, and no one more so than Malcolm, for he learned from these broadcasts what policy decisions were being made at the national headquarters and how they would affect the other temples in the Nation. Malcolm had taught us that proper listening required as much skill as speaking, so we'd sit exceptionally still and concentrate totally on the words of the Messenger. It reminded me of times as a child when we'd be sitting in church or Sunday school listening to the preacher and it seemed you didn't dare even to flicker an eyelid because the slightest movement a child might make would invite for sure the evil eye of everyone else in the pew, or when a summer day broke into a thunderstorm and everyone would sit stock-still in a room and you thought that if you even breathed lightning would be sure to strike you.

NOI matters were also discussed with Malcolm over coffee or snacks, and sometimes over dinner, too, at the temple restaurant. Sister Lana, our cook, braised lamb shanks better than anyone in the Muslim world, Malcolm claimed. Sister Lana eventually left the temple restaurant to cook for Muhammad Ali and later for Mr. Muhammad in Chicago, but she started out with us at Number Seven in New York. Each day she would prepare two or three specials as well as a ton of rice and vegetables for our evening meal, and during the day she'd have a variety of freshly made juices—celery, apple, carrot, cabbage—to offer us as snacks. She'd have fresh fruit on hand, too, and bean pie. She made a good strong cup of coffee. (Malcolm drank a lot of coffee, with milk.) Occasionally I might sneak into the restaurant with another of the assistants for what was not permitted, a big breakfast of eggs fried up with Sister Lana's homemade Salaam beef sausage.

The temple restaurant was small, but Sister Lana still needed help serving the tables. Other Muslim sisters worked with her as waitresses. Like most waitresses, they relied on tips for their living. Malcolm never stinted when it came to tipping, he appreciated people's services, but one waitress at the restaurant really began to trouble him. Solemnly she would take his order; with no dallying she would bring him his cup of coffee and maybe a tiny piece of bean pie. But she would never smile. Malcolm mentioned this to several of us at the restaurant one day and expressed some concern about her welfare. We realized, when we began thinking about it, that none of us had ever seen her smile, either. She served us efficiently, but she seemed always to be so sober, almost glum. Her manner was probably costing her good tips. We decided to mention Malcolm's concern to her. We also started offering her some pointers about tips and service with a smile. She listened to us, only the more we talked the sadder she grew and it hurt to look into her soft, dark eyes. When we had finished, she answered reluctantly that the reason she never smiled was because all the teeth in the front of her mouth were rotten. And she didn't have the money to pay for a dentist. Embarrassed by our uninformed presumptions, we reported back to Malcolm. The next Sunday he made a sermon of our experience and then took up a collection that enabled us to send the waitress who never smiled to a dentist.

The waitress at 22 West, a coffee shop on 135th Street, would greet Malcolm with both a smile and an ice-cream scoop. Malcolm liked the conversation at 22 West, a spot popular among African-American professionals, civil-rights leaders, and intellectuals—people like the journalist Louis Lomax or comedian Dick Gregory or Roy Wilkins, the head of the Urban League in Harlem. Although I'd often hear Malcolm call some of the people who frequented the coffee shop Uncle Toms, he would nevertheless seem always to find their company stimulating. "Mind sharpens mind like stone sharpens knife," Malcolm used to say, quoting a Chinese proverb, and he wanted to keep the blade of his mind well honed. Malcolm also liked the banana splits at 22 West. Before he'd even be settled in his booth at the back of the restaurant, the waitress would be topping three huge scoops of vanilla ice cream with either pineapple or butterscotch sauce (but no nuts) and a mountain of whipped cream. Malcolm didn't even have to order, and when she brought the sundae to our table, Malcolm's wide, contagious smile would light up the whole place from the back of the back booth all the way up to the front door. ("Always face the door," Malcolm often said, and always did. "You know how Wild Bill Hickok got it.")

Malcolm's weakness for banana splits did not prevent him from keeping his lanky body lean and trim. Sister Betty used to say he looked malnourished. Malcolm, though, would not have allowed himself to be undernourished any more than he would ever have let himself get overweight. Obesity repelled Malcolm. He saw it as a case of self-indulgence unchecked by self-discipline. He often spoke out against it at the Sunday meetings as well as in his lectures to both the MGT (Muslim Girls Training) and the FOI (Fruit of Islam). He once ordered the MGT to go out and buy scales so that they could regularly weigh themselves. He also told those sisters who were already overweight that he'd give them two weeks' time to lose ten pounds—and that if they failed, he'd give them time out; he meant a suspension. At an FOI meeting, referring to two of the larger brothers, Malcolm said he didn't like sitting between them because their bodies overheated the atmosphere and they soaked up all the oxygen in the air. Malcolm never said these things privately—Malcolm never said anything privately—because inside the temple we had no secrets. Words were not spoken about you behind your back; they were spoken in public, in front of everyone, so that if you erred or strayed from Muslim discipline, you erred in front of everyone. It kept you on your toes. At a Sunday service, before hundreds of brothers and sisters, Malcolm might say, "Sister Catherine Joseph, you're getting too heavy again, you need to lose that excess weight," and then he'd speak a lesson about will power and temptation. You would soon realize he was talking about more than eating three meals a day or sneaking into the temple restaurant for one of Sister Lana's breakfast specials.

We fasted three days each month. Fasts began on Friday morning and ended on Sunday evening, when we would be allowed to eat again. Our fasts did not merely provide us with an exercise in self-control. They also cleansed us. In three days the system was purged of all waste matter, the blood was purified, and the brain was freshly supplied with oxygen. You would lose some weight, too. The primary purpose of our fasts, however, was spiritual enlightenment. Throughout the fast we would not miss a single of our five daily Islamic prayers, and we would read from the Koran.

Most important, we would turn our minds to some spiritual objective, we'd train all our thoughts on it, so as to lose ourselves in contemplation and raise the level of our spiritual awareness. I don't know what spiritual heights Malcolm may have reached during those fasts, but I do know that I have never seen a light in any human face like the one I'd see radiating from his by the time we reached our third day, or like the beam in his eyes, and you'd never see it any other time.

Everyone fasted, except those sisters who were menstruating or pregnant. Travel also exempted you from fasts, as did illness. If you became ill during the course of a fast, you were expected to break the fast immediately and eat. One story Malcolm loved to tell concerned a zealous young brother—he had just received his X—who undertook his first fast with more confidence than sense. Malcolm suggested to the new brother that he might want to start off gradually and fast for only one day, or perhaps two, his first time. (About the middle of the second day, after your body has been deprived of all solid food and any liquids other than water, coffee, or tea for thirty-six hours, a fast can become a little bit frightening. You begin to feel as if your body belongs to a stranger, and crazy things may start going on inside your head.) Undeterred, the young brother insisted he could make it through all three days. On a hot, summery Sunday morning, the third day, when he awoke, the overeager brother found his body too weak to get him out of bed. Alarm bells began ringing in his head. Panicked, sweating, he managed to roll off the bed and onto the floor. Leading with his elbows, he succeeded in dragging himself across the floor over to the window. He grabbed hold of the windowsill. He pulled; and when he had pulled up enough of himself so that he could holler out the open window, he did. He started hollering down to the people on the street that he was dying. "Food! Food!" he kept crying, sure that any minute he'd be dead without it. While Malcolm respected the determination and enthusiasm the new brother had exhibited, he used his case to teach us as a lesson in blind confidence and extremism. The brother had tried, but he had tried wrongly. He had failed to pursue his goal at a moderate pace that would gain him the experience to succeed. Malcolm did find it humorous, though. "Food, food," he would say again, and laugh. Malcolm had a rich, full laugh—not loud but full—and he'd slap the side of his thigh, as if he couldn't contain himself, so you felt it was his whole body laughing, and his soul.

You have to keep your body fit to contain your soul, Malcolm would tell us. Walking, mostly, kept Malcolm fit, and the many people he knew or would meet on Harlem's streets —the storekeepers, businessmen, mothers and children, the clergy, panhandlers—kept his spirits high. Malcolm walked like a racehorse. I'd often walk with him from the temple on 116th Street up to 22 West or just about anywhere in Harlem, and once he'd struck his stride, I'd always have difficulty keeping pace with him, even though we stood about the same height. For me, walking with Malcolm, observing and listening to him with the people on the street, provided the happiest kind of exercise.

The FOI provided more formal exercise. Without exception, all Muslim men were required to participate in the FOI, which included Captain Joseph's program in martial arts. Captain Joseph, who headed the FOI at Number Seven, conducted our military drills and calisthenics. He also trained us in martial arts. Though military in its organization and discipline, the FOI instructed us only in combat techniques that did not employ weapons. It developed our instincts, our pride, our stamina. It taught us to rely upon our own individual strength, a strength multiplied a thousandfold inside an Islamic regiment. Captain Joseph was making sure that we'd be ready for the War of Armageddon. He made better men of lesser men. He took the new brothers—men who had just left a secular community where they may have been abusing their minds and bodies with drugs or alcohol—and indefatigably he reformed them. He made of them the Fruit of Islam.

The temple had a chain of command. Whereas the assistant ministers reported to Malcolm, and he to Mr. Muhammad, all the other FOI members reported to Captain Joseph, whose immediate superior was not Malcolm but Supreme Captain Raymond Sharrieff in Chicago. When reporting to Captain Joseph, a brother would first salute the crescent flag that hung beside a photograph of the Honorable Elijah Muhammad. Next he would salute Captain Joseph and, after the salute had been returned, the lieutenant on duty. The captain would then give the brother his assignment of the day. The captain determined which brothers would do advance security checks wherever the minister might be speaking, and he decided who would serve as bodyguards to Malcolm and who would flank any other officials or special visitors. Captain Joseph also designated the uniform of the day—what color suit, shirt, tie, socks, shoes—for Malcolm's assistants as well as the FOI, and any deviation had to be cleared through him. If you showed up in your navy blue suit with a striped blue tie instead of the designated red one, you'd better have a good reason, because Captain Joseph was not a gentle man.

A dress code governed the sisters, too, although you'd not always know it by the look of some of them. Even if they did hem their dresses at the prescribed length, some of the new sister members would pull their ample bodices in tight around their waists just to raise their skirts that inch or so more and to show they had a figure. These sisters would probably also be wearing gaudy jewelry. They would plaster on the lipstick, and they'd have dyed their hair so often and so many different shades you'd have no idea what nature had intended. The sight of them could rile Malcolm. He encouraged them to wear looser, flowing garments, clothes that were tastefully designed but also colorful; Malcolm took no pleasure in the dowdy or drab. Black women who bared their knees and hid their natural hair, however, belonged not in Temple Number Seven, he would say, but with the devil's own kind. They were imitating the styles and fads of white women, he would say, and imitation is bondage. The white man's Madison Avenue advertising had robbed these sisters of their true esteem and had bound their minds in chains. Whether you're wearing iron chains or mental ones doesn't matter, Malcolm would say, you're still a slave.

You might think some of those flashy sisters were simply trying to attract the attentions of one of the brothers, but in fact the temple allowed almost no direct contact between the sisters and the brothers, especially the unmarried ones. No single people, for instance, were permitted to dance at our social affairs, and married men could dance only with their wives. This rule was sometimes met with resistance because most of the brothers loved to dance, and not just with their wives. Malcolm would help them to see reason. What would you do, Malcolm would ask them, if you happened to walk into a club and you saw your wife standing there in the arms of another man. Then he'd ask them why it should make any difference that your wife and another man were standing in the middle of the floor with their arms wrapped around each other and their bodies pressed close together just because there was music playing.

In the Muslim community no man was allowed to touch any woman in any way unless he was married to her. So there was no dating between Muslim men and women, no courtship in any conventional sense, and certainly no sampling. Anyone who engaged in sex before marriage or outside it was suspended from the Nation for one year. The Nation did of course have procedures for those single men and women who might be seriously interested in each other. For a brother the channel of communication with a Muslim woman was the sister captain of the MGT; a sister, on the other hand, directed her inquiries to the brother captain of the

FOI. If a sister expressed her interest in a particular brother
to Captain Joseph, for example, he would speak with the
man in question. If the brother was likewise interested, the
captain would provide the woman with detailed information
regarding the brother's residence, his family background,
his education and occupation, his personal history before
joining the NOI, and his personal habits. The sister captain
would provide the brother with similar information. This
process could continue until the brother and sister arrived at
a mutual agreement to marry. The proposed marriage then
had to be publicly announced in the temple several weeks
prior to the ceremony, and not until after the marriage were
the brother and sister allowed to be in each other's company
without a chaperone—not in anyone's home, not in the temple, not in a restaurant or any other public place. Our community had its rules, but it didn't have teenage pregnancies,
or babies born out of wedlock, or adultery, and in all my
years at the temple I remember only one divorce.

All Muslims honor marriage. Marriage builds families, and
in the family lies the strength of the Nation. Malcolm constantly exhorted the married brothers and sisters at Temple
Number Seven to increase the black Muslim nation. He
urged them to multiply its number with children born
healthy and raised Muslim, children whose minds would
never know the enslavement of a white Christian society. We
therefore did not practice birth control, and we placed serious importance upon prenatal care. Tobacco and alcohol
and drugs were of course forbidden all members of the NOI,
but Malcolm also encouraged pregnant sisters to eat proper
foods, to drink healthful fruit and vegetable juices, to get
proper sleep, and to think proper thoughts. He strongly recommended that they avoid activities like visits to the zoo or
watching horror movies because they might be startled or
frightened and in turn traumatize the child in the womb. He
advised them to exercise in order to make the birthing easier.
He instructed them to avoid arguments of any kind so as not

to bear a nervous child. Malcolm also counseled the husbands not to upset their pregnant wives with domestic squabbles or heated arguments or any threatening behavior that could adversely affect the child, because the child might turn around in the womb and strangle itself in the umbilical cord. Malcolm also had some things to say about nursing the child after its birth. Breastfeeding, he said, provided the child with essential immunities and nutrients not supplied by cow's milk, which might strengthen the child's bones but not much else. He pointed out, too, that breastfeeding put the baby's ear close to the mother's heartbeat. The heart beats like a drum—"boom-boom, boom-boom," he'd illustrate—and this constant, regular heartbeat pacifies the child, whose security is further enhanced by the warm embrace of its mother's arms. A baby lying in a cradle with a bottle of formula, on the other hand, is being denied comfort, wonder, nourishment, and trust. Ninety-nine percent of the women at Number Seven nursed their children at their breasts.

Everything changed when you entered the Nation of Islam, everything from the food you put into your mouth to the words that came out of it. Profanity was forbidden. We did not curse or use vulgar language, nor did we expose ourselves to it. That's why movies with explicit sex scenes and coarse speech and so-called adult themes were not allowed. That's why the jukebox in the temple restaurant played only African or Middle Eastern music, and some jazz, but no blues and no rock-and-roll with its uninspiring music and often downright dirty lyrics. Forbidden, too, were gossip and the slandering of any brother's or sister's name. Slight talk can divide people. The FBI knew that, and Malcolm knew they knew. To stir up trouble and create contention within our close community the FBI would instruct one of its informants to start dropping hints about how some brother with a bit of spare cash and time was supposedly hanging around another brother's wife, and you'd soon be witnessing exactly what the FBI wanted: divisiveness and disunity. So in the temple you gossiped at your own risk—and to your embarrassment. Malcolm saw to that.

One day at the temple one of the new young brothers, a college-educated professional, snickered at the frayed dress one of the poorer sisters was wearing; he then passed a snide comment about the worn-down and run-over condition of her shoes. As the brother had only recently joined the temple, he may not have been fully aware of the seriousness of his offense. He learned soon enough. He was not only reprimanded severely by both Malcolm and Captain Joseph but also made the subject of Malcolm's Sunday lesson. Malcolm questioned why the young man should be following one of the sisters with his eyes in the first place, and then only to laugh at her. And why, Malcolm asked, should he be making judgments about this good young woman on the basis of her clothes and shoes. It prompted one of Malcolm's parables.

Malcolm told us of a man who had been blessed with very productive farmland. A stream ran through the center of his land and in its fertile soil grew corn and grapes and pomegranates in great abundance. His crops made him rich, and vain. He bragged often of his bountiful harvests to his neighbor, a far less fortunate farmer, and he would laugh at the poor man's few parched stalks of corn. One day the poor man told the rich farmer that instead of bragging about his great fortune he should be thanking God for blessing him with such rich soil and for irrigating his land with a stream and for providing his crops with rain. The poor man told the thankless farmer to consider what might happen if God were to send down a torrent on his land. Its waters would swallow up his crops as its winds would blow them down, in the sodden earth their roots would rot, and the rich man would be left with nothing. And a torrent did come. The stream overran its banks, it drowned the corn and grapes and pomegranates, it flooded the land. The once blessed farmer wrung his hands. He cried and moaned his lot; he grieved that he had not praised God, as had his poor neighbor, for his harvest. The poor man meanwhile came to great wealth. He listened long to the other man's woes. Then he told him it was no better to grieve loss than to boast wealth, for only through God do we gain.

And the young brother who had laughed at the poor woman's shoes was taught humility by Malcolm's parable. He went out and he bought the poor sister a new pair of shoes. He gave them to Brother Captain Joseph, who passed them on to the sister captain. She passed them on to the good young sister. A message accompanied the new pair of shoes. Information was exchanged. A proposal followed. The sister said yes. Banns were posted. After they were married, the young brother sent his new wife to college. She wanted to become a lawyer. These kinds of things happened inside the temple.

"Islam gave me wings."

Louis Lomax tells the story in *When the Word Is Given* of Malcolm's attempt to convert a black man of the Baptist faith to the teachings of Islam. Interested, the Baptist asked Malcolm what were the rules of the NOI.

"Well, my brother, you have to stop drinking, stop swearing, stop gambling, stop using dope, and stop cheating on your wife," Malcolm answered.

"Hell," the Baptist rejoindered, "I think I had better remain a Christian."

From the moment that Malcolm converted to Islam in a Massachusetts maximum-security prison to the day he died by assassins' bullets at the Audubon Ballroom he was governed willingly by the strict morality of the NOI. Having radically altered his own personal habits in his pursuit of Islamic righteousness, he expected no less of those sisters and brothers who chose to follow him out of the North American wilderness into the Muslim nation. In his moral principles, as in his table manners, he set them a meticulous example. He was, says Lomax, "the most puritanical man I ever met."

Of all the stories Malcolm would tell during the course of his Muslim ministry to make a moral point, none would be more compelling than his own. It was the story of the resourceful but restless black youth who plummeted into the depths of criminal depravity on steamy city streets and was serving a ten-year prison term in a state penitentiary by the time he was twenty. It was the story of a fallen man who heard the words of the Messenger Elijah Muhammad in the dead light of his prison cell, and in them discovered the Muslim path out of moral darkness to redemption and rebirth. It was a story of death and life. Out of his personal history Malcolm wove a dramatic metaphor for the miracle of Islam.

* * *

Often at the temple we would speak of the dead, but we weren't talking about black people who had in fact died and been buried in a cemetery, *says Benjamin Karim,* we were talking about "the so-called American negroes" who lived in ignorance of themselves and their condition. We might also call them the deaf, dumb, and blind because the so-called American negroes failed to use their senses—or their sense—in dealing with the white society that was continually oppressing them. Like Lazarus who lay full of sores outside his master's gate and begged for the crumbs from his master's table, they were willing to wait until they died and went to heaven to receive their just reward. And it was black preachers in Christian churches who taught them that to ensure their heavenly reward they had to worship at the altar of a white man's religion on Sunday and every other day submit their will to that of the white slavemaster himself. Talk about the blind leading the blind. Preachers and parishioners alike, they were all of them mentally dead. Malcolm taught many lessons on this subject.

Etymology was one of Malcolm's favorite teaching methods. At one of our public meetings at the temple, I remember, he picked up his piece of chalk and wrote the letter *N* on the blackboard. *N*, he spoke it out, and *e*, *g*, *r*, and *o* likewise followed. *Negro*, he said, like all words, has an origin and a history. Words have roots that may lie in ancient times —in ancient tongues like Hebrew, Arabic, Latin, and Greek —and their meanings may change in the course of time; a word's ancestry is its etymology. Malcolm then pointed to the blackboard and explained that the English word *negro*, like the French word *nègre*, comes to us from the Spanish word *negro*, which means "black" or "dark." Its roots, though, go much farther back in history, all the way back to the ancient Latin word for dark or black, which is *niger*—and which didn't ever also mean "nigger." Again speaking out the letters as he chalked them onto the blackboard, Malcolm wrote the Latin word *necro*. *Necro*, he told us, had its roots in the even more ancient Greek word *nekros*, meaning "the dead" or "a corpse." Next he told us that the Greek word for city was *polis*, and he wrote it out on the blackboard right behind *necro*, to make the word *necropolis*. In these two Greek words, then, lie the origins of the English word *necropolis*, which is a cemetery, a city of the dead. Malcolm then asked us to consider that the word *negropolis* would therefore signify a city of black people or so-called American negroes, which is practically the same thing as a necropolis— all you need to do is close the *c* and put a hook on it to make a *g*—because a city of so-called American negroes is a city of dead people no matter how you look at it. You only have to look at their necks, said Malcolm. These black people don't just put crosses on their graves, they also wear them around their necks. So, Malcolm concluded, whenever you see a so- called American negro with a cross around his neck, you know he's dead from there on up. This comment, unexpected as it was, cracked everyone up, just as Malcolm intended it to do. It was one of his teaching methods to raise your anger with insults one minute and to crack you up the next.

Malcolm wanted to unbury the dead. Before entering the temple, I, like most of the brothers and sisters, had been an occasional churchgoer. In New York I had not joined any one particular Christian church because I found no solace in the hollow words of our black Christian preachers. They spoke not so much to our souls, it seemed to me, as they did to our wallets and pocketbooks. They spoke numbers; they wanted to build their congregations, they wanted to build bigger churches, they wanted to bank bigger collections. And they never spoke to our intelligence. With fatherly distance they treated us like children and expected us to be either grateful or happy. "Now's the time to get happy," they'd say, "so let's get happy. Get happy, get happy!" and they'd start the dancing and the shouting and the tambourines so that we would forget exactly what we should have been remembering—the misery and the pain we had known one hour earlier and every day for four hundred years before. Nor would their so-called heaven change any of that, not if you believed the church walls that everywhere pictured parties of serenely unconcerned angels rising above billowy white clouds into radiant light and placid skies—and everywhere every angel's skin, like every angel's wing, was oppressively white. My churchgoing days had become rarer by the time I first visited Number Seven, but still my mind was bound by church teachings, and even if my small-time gambling didn't much trouble my conscience, I was getting to be lost more and more to the city streets. Like many brothers before me and many brothers since, I needed to be found.

Malcolm rescued us from the myth of our moral inferiority. To achieve our Muslim selfhood we had to stop cursing and swearing, give up smoking and drinking and cardsharping and gambling, quit using drugs or peddling them, quit hustling, and refrain from chasing after women. At the same time we were of course adopting the lifestyle of the Muslim community. We changed. Malcolm restored to us our self-esteem. He enlightened us; he brought the mentally dead back to consciousness.

Guided by the wisdom Malcolm had gained from his personal experience, all of us in our own way underwent a transformation like Malcolm's own. Malcolm shared with us the story of his former life, when he was a teenager going from bad to worse on Harlem's streets. Restless, unable to hold a job any steadier than portering from city to city on

the New Haven Railroad line, he took to hustling and peddling dope, pot mostly—but he wouldn't deal drugs with
kids, they didn't do that then, and he wasn't involved in any
killings. Theft and burglary eventually landed him in prison.
He had wasted every year of his teens. He had not in any
constructive way used or developed his intelligence since
he'd left school after the eighth grade. If he had not been
arrested in Boston for larceny, he said, he would have
wasted the rest of his life as well. He said he would have been
as good as dead.

Prison at first intensified Malcolm's restlessness. With
thoughts only of release or escape he paced the confines of
his prison cell. He was like the lion in a cage; give him a
spoon and he'd dig his way out. On visiting days, with his
younger brother Reginald, he spoke constantly of getting out
or going mad. Reginald, a Muslim, suggested that he study
Islam to help set his mind free. Malcolm read some of the
NOI literature, and he also met an inmate from Detroit Temple Number One who explained to him the teachings of Elijah Muhammad. Malcolm converted to the Muslim faith, and
from that day on he set out to achieve righteousness, for only
when he had cleansed himself in body, mind, and spirit
would he be worthy of Allah.

In Islam Malcolm found his focus, and he went crazy with
it. Everything he read was new, and everything new excited
him, so he was continually being sent off in yet other new
directions. He was reading every minute he could find. He
started reading the dictionary at A, although he didn't really
know where he was going with it—except to Z. Learning
charged him. Charged in so many different directions at
once, however, he was directionless. An old white man in the
prison, a Mason, put Malcolm straight. He told Malcolm a
story of three men who got lost in a jungle. When night fell
upon them with total darkness, they panicked. They stumbled in the darkness and fell down. Each one scrambled to
grab hold of some object for security in the dark. One man

pulled himself up from the ground and cried out to his comrades that he was hanging on to a rope. A second man shouted that he was clinging to the trunk of a tree. The third one said that he had hold of something like a hose. When the day broke, though, the three men discovered they were all holding on to the same thing. An elephant.

Malcolm never forgot that old white Mason or his story. It made him realize that he, too, had caught hold of something but that he had no idea whatever of either its nature or its magnitude. It taught him to curb his excitement with patience, strategy, thought, procedures. For the next six years in three different prisons he pursued his studies methodically, explored each part that would help him define a whole, only to discover that whole was yet another part. He read all day in the prison library. He trained himself to sleep less at night, and after lights out he read by the light that came from the hallway through the bars of his prison cell. He made up for his lost years and strained his eyes so badly he had to get glasses.

Being unreformed by Islam is like being dead. In prison, Malcolm told us, he found his salvation, because in prison he discovered Islam, which gave him a new life. Prison was Malcolm's cocoon. Inside it he reformed and educated himself. Malcolm shed one life form so a new one could be born. Malcolm called it his metamorphosis. Just as the caterpillar is transformed into a butterfly inside its cocoon, the drug peddler, street hustler, and larcenist emerged from prison as Malcolm X.

All of us who entered the temple underwent our own kind of metamorphosis. All of us understood what Malcolm had meant when he had said, shortly after his release from prison: "Islam gave me wings."

Inside the Temple

A placard on the 116th Street storefront housing the New York temple notified the general public that the Nation of Islam met in the auditorium upstairs at 2 P.M. every Sunday and at 8 P.M. on Wednesday and Friday. The notice provided the barest outline of the activity at Temple Number Seven.

The Sunday meetings, which were open to the public, began promptly at two o'clock with a lecture by one of the assistant ministers. The assistant minister would also introduce the temple's spiritual guide, Brother Minister Malcolm, who would deliver the main address to the brothers and sisters of Temple Number Seven. Malcolm always had a message, too, for the unconverted among his growing congregations. He strove to awaken their black consciousness and encouraged them to join unto their own kind. Those who wished no longer to be numbered among the lost but to take their place among the lost-found in the Nation of Islam were invited to attend the Wednesday evening meeting at which assistant ministers oriented new members to the ways of the Nation. The recently lost and newly found were welcome at the temple on Friday evenings as well, for General Civilization Night, when Malcolm spoke less formally than he did at his Sunday lectures on a variety of topics from What Is Civilization to Table Etiquette.

* * *

Friday night at the temple was called General Civilization Night, *Benjamin Karim explains*, because Malcolm would always start off the meeting with a big question from one of our Muslim lessons. "What is civilization?" he might ask, or "What is the duty of a civilized man?" He might end up, however, talking about breastfeeding or eating bean pie. Diet, language, table manners, liturgy, scriptures, polished shoes, they are all parts of the same elephant, and each part reveals something of a whole that you might call civilization. You can tell a lot about a person, Malcolm often said, not only by what he eats but also by how he eats it. Modes of conduct as much as schools of thought reflect a person's culture, he taught us, and a person's culture reflects a people's culture. For generations, he pointed out, black people in America have been divorced from their native culture, so the history of African Americans in the United States has become a history of losses. When our ancestors were transplanted to America four centuries ago by their white slavemasters, they were fed bad meat, they were lashed by foreign tongues, and they were drugged with Christianity. Generation by generation they died and forgot or lost more of their traditions, language, religion, and culture, until black Americans in the middle of the twentieth century were believing their ancestors had swung like Tarzan and the apes on tropical vines through the jungle or had boiled missionaries alive in caldrons for their dinner. Without culture, Malcolm said, you are a savage, and with the white man's culture you are a slave. He made us realize we were neither slave nor savage, for we had a rich African heritage, history, and continent. Four hundred years in America, though, had so crippled us with pain and numbed us to injustices that we had to gasp for one free breath. When you have patients that close to death, Malcolm said, you rush them into Emergency. The NOI, he said, is the emergency room for all of us who have been disenfranchised and dispossessed by white America. Each Friday he would help us see some of the many ways the NOI restored to us what we were being continually denied: our true civilization.

Had Malcolm started a Friday meeting by asking who was the Father of Civilization, any member of the FOI would have responded without blinking, and probably without comprehending the full significance of his reply, that it was the Asiatic Black Man. Malcolm, however, was not looking for rote replies. He wanted us to think; he taught us to reason out how abstract ideas applied to our daily lives. The FOI, on the other hand, required us to memorize, and in the first of five NOI lesson plans, which all FOI members had to learn word for word, appeared the question "Who Is the Original Man?" Its answer was "The Asiatic Black Man, Owner, Maker, Cream of the Planet Earth, Father of Civilization, God of the Universe." Not until we had proved our mastery of the NOI catechism by memorizing and reciting perfectly every question and answer, every statement, proposition, and problem in all five of the lesson plans was our membership in the Fruit of Islam fully ratified.

Under the heading Student Enrollment, the first of the five lesson plans included twelve questions and answers that dealt with the origins of human history and civilization. We were taught why, for example, the white devil was settled in Europe: "Because the earth belongs to the Original Black Man, and knowing that the devil was wicked, He put him in the worst part and kept the best part preserved for Himself." Lesson Number One followed with a series of fourteen questions and answers regarding the historical and ideological battle between Islam and Christianity. "Why did we take Jerusalem from the devil?" asks one question, which is answered "Because our righteous brother by the name of Jesus was buried there and they use his name to shield their dirty religion called Christianity. We took Jerusalem from the devil seven hundred and fifty years ago." Next, the one-page English Lesson C1 presents a statement written by W.D.

Fard, the Prophet and founder in 1930 of the NOI, as well as questions about the so-called negroes' childhood fear of the white man (because the devil gave them the wrong food to eat when they were babies) and their love of the white man now that they've grown (because the devil gives them nothing). Twenty more questions and answers comprise Lesson Number Two, and the last of the five lesson plans, the Problem Book, explains "the problem of the so-called negro in a mathematical way."

In the case of the fifth lesson plan we had to memorize thirty-four mind-boggling problems and then attempt to solve them. One problem presented us with the volume of water in Lake Michigan and then asked us to determine how long it would take thirteen ducks, each of them drinking a particular amount of water each day, to drink Lake Michigan dry. The ducks in Lake Michigan were followed by a lion in a cage that measured two thousand miles wide and three thousand miles long. With modern equipment, we were told, the lion was able to walk sixty feet per minute. Given that, we were asked to calculate how long it would take the lion to walk the perimeter of the cage and how long it would take him to find the door. The problems had a metaphoric point. The lion, for instance, represented the African-American people and the cage America itself. Equipped with knowledge from the Nation of Islam, the lion could hasten his pace and more quickly discover the door that would lead him out of his cage. "Hurry, hurry," the Problem Book exhorted us, "study all that you can. There is a big world awaiting the wide-awake man," it continued, and said, "Islam is mathematics and mathematics is Islam. It stands true to reason and can be proven in no limit of time."

We might be called upon to recite any part of our catechism any Monday night at the weekly meetings of the Fruit of Islam. Only members of the FOI, which included all Muslim brothers, were allowed in the temple on FOI nights. Contrary to media propaganda, we were not an elite paramilitary corps or death squad or special karate unit. Some brothers were trained in karate, it is true, and martial arts were taught, but mainly to provide us with the lessons in self-defense, self-discipline, and self-control that we needed to be worthy of our name. We were the fruit of the tree of Islam, which had been planted in Arabia by Muhammad thirteen hundred years ago. Its roots had spread across North Africa; it had flourished all the way from Spain to the Indus Valley, and had grown as far east as Indonesia, but not until the twentieth century did the tree of Islam reach America. In Detroit in the 1930s it bore new fruit, and in the black Nation of Islam founded by Fard will the promise of Muslim dominion over all the earth be fulfilled.

On Monday nights, too, the FOI court held sessions to hear charges against any members who may have violated the laws of the Muslim community. Violations carried suspensions, the nature of the violation determining the length of the suspension. Less serious offenses like smoking a cigarette or using profanity in front of a woman carried suspensions of thirty or sixty days, whereas a brother who committed adultery would be suspended for five years (he could apply for reinstatement after one, however). For criminal offenses like robbery we did not take such drastic measures as cutting off the guilty party's fingers or hand, but the offender could be suspended for up to five years. If the FOI was holding court, Malcolm attended the meeting. Once the charges had been heard, if the defendant pleaded guilty, Malcolm would announce the sentence. If the defendant pleaded innocent, Malcolm would hear the arguments of both the defendant and the accuser, and then sentence one or the other of them. If a defendant was found to be falsely charged, the accuser was suspended for the period of time stipulated by the violation he had reported to the court. Whoever the party, whatever his position, Malcolm never displayed favoritism in these matters; his gavel fell on all with equal weight.

One month or one year, suspensions were more painful than they may initially appear to be to an outsider. Suspension denied you all contact with your brothers and sisters in the Muslim community. It excluded you not only from their social activities but also from their care, responsibility, and trust. It deprived you of any real sense of community and cost you your sense of security, because you didn't merely believe Islam—you lived it. Having totally adopted a Muslim lifestyle, you could not easily rejoin mainstream Christian society. Nor could you join a temple in another city, as the temple secretary there would contact national headquarters to ascertain whether you were a member in good standing. During the term of a suspension you were expected to teach what you had learned to people who had not yet heard the message of Islam. During this period, too, your activities were monitored by an FOI investigator. He would report any further violations of Muslim law back to the temple or attest to your good behavior. If neither the investigator nor any other NOI member voiced new charges before the court, you were welcomed back into the Muslim community with applause. Nor was your particular case ever again mentioned; you were forgiven and your misdemeanor forgotten. An exoneration gladdened a Monday night at the FOI.

Saturday mornings brought the children in the Muslim community to the temple, often for outings with Malcolm, in which case they would congregate with high expectations and bag lunches. Malcolm liked to take the temple children to the Museum of Natural History or the Hayden Planetarium. He would excite them with the prospect of learning something new and unusual as he'd usher them through the museum halls. Wide-eyed, they would gather around an exhibit on dinosaurs or the Eskimo. Museums are our schools, Malcolm used to say, and standing in front of an exhibit, he would turn the visit into an instructive class. He would talk to the children in their own language about how the harsh arctic climate of the Far North affected the lives of Eskimos. He'd

The Honorable Elijah Muhammad, Messenger of Allah and Dear Holy Apostle, leads an NOI prayer meeting at Griffith Stadium in Washington, D.C., on September 10, 1961. *UPI/Bettmann*

Malcolm at an NOI dinner with Minister Wallace, Elijah Muhammad's second son: "an honest man, a humble man, whose integrity had always set him outside the circle of power in Chicago." *New York Amsterdam News Photo*

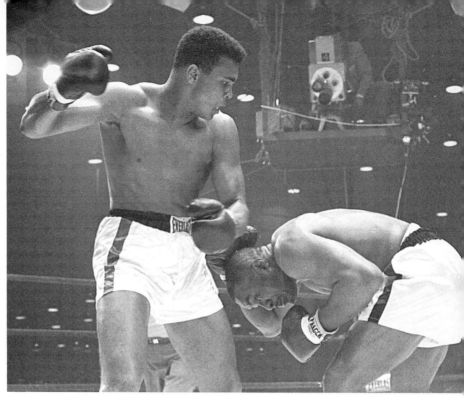

Cassius Clay (later Muhammad Ali) overpowering Sonny Liston for the world championship title in Miami on February 25, 1964. Malcolm, then Clay's spiritual adviser, attended the match. *UPI/Bettmann*

"In Chicago the NOI officials were calling Malcolm X a hypocrite. Louis Farrakhan in Boston was calling him a hypocrite. . . . In every issue of *Muhammad Speaks* someone was calling Malcolm a hypocrite." Louis Farrakhan surrounded by bodyguards addresses a rally in 1985. *UPI/Bettmann*

Malcolm at his house in Queens after it was firebombed on February 14, 1965:
"Around 2:45 A.M. the interior of Malcolm's house burst into flames that endangered
the lives not only of Malcolm and Sister Betty but also of [their four daughters]
ranging in age from six months to six years." *UPI/Bettmann*

Outside the Audubon Ballroom in Harlem, the scene of the assassination of Malcolm X on Sunday, February 21, 1965. *UPI/Bettmann*

Outside the Audubon Ballroom, just after the assassination; Malcolm on gurney. He was pronounced dead on arrival at Columbia-Presbyterian Hospital at 3:30 P.M., February 21, 1965. *UPI/Bettmann*

"When I walked back out on the stage [after the assassination] everyone had left the Audubon. My eyes scanned a deserted ballroom, an empty stage, the podium, the microphone, an overturned chair." *UPI/Bettmann Newsphoto*

Ossie Davis presides over memorial service for Malcolm on February 27, 1965. "He praised 'our own shining black Prince,' [but] did not capture the man I knew: the minister, from the Latin word for servant; our counselor, healer, judge, and peacemaker; the teacher at the blackboard with a world in his mind and a piece of chalk in his hand." *UPI/Bettmann*

point out that Eskimos had no forests or mines, so they had no wood or metal to make tools. Then he'd get the children to tell him that Eskimos were surrounded by the sea and that the sea provided them with fish to eat. And what else? Malcolm would ask, and talk to them about sea animals like the walrus, whose bones and tusks were carved by the Eskimos into clubs and knives and fish hooks and combs. All at the same time the kids would want to see the display of Eskimo implements. From exhibit to exhibit Malcolm would capture the attention of not only the kids from the temple but other kids, too, black and white, and some of them would be perched up on their parents' shoulders so they could see. Malcolm attracted crowds. His teaching had universal appeal. He inspired these seven-, nine-, ten-, and twelve-year-olds to think for themselves, to explore, to ask questions, to read.

Malcolm wanted our Muslim children to cultivate their minds. One Saturday morning at the temple he wrote the German word *Kinder* on the blackboard and explained to his eager young audience that *Kinder* was the German word for what they were: children. When he attached the word *Garten* to it, the children leapt at the chance to tell Malcolm what a kindergarten was. Malcolm, however, wanted to know why a kindergarten was called what it was. He asked them what they supposed the German word *Garten* meant. One child said garden, and several others chimed in that a kindergarten was a garden for children. Another added it was a garden where children grow. All smiles, Malcolm congratulated his Saturday kids. Children are *like* gardens, too, he told them, for there is no place more fertile than a child's mind and in its rich soil all sorts of possibilities grow. Malcolm often would say that children's minds were like cups waiting to be filled, whereas the minds of adults had become so cluttered with problems and prejudice that they distorted knowledge, resisted new ideas, and deflected enlightenment. In our children and in education Malcolm saw our hope.

That's why he urged Muslim children to study their school-books and to use their leisure time creatively, to spend a Saturday at a museum rather than sitting in the bleachers at a football game or watching sports on television. You don't see thousands of Jews lining up for tickets to a basketball or football game, Malcolm used to tell us, because Jews value education and learning more than anything else. Because they eat grass, he'd say, is no reason why we should eat dirt. You don't throw out the baby with the bath water, he'd say.

Saturday night was Unity Night at the temple. Unity Nights afforded the families in our Muslim community as well as the single brothers and sisters an opportunity to socialize in a cordial, relaxed atmosphere. There would be refreshments; we'd talk, we'd listen to music. The jukebox in the temple restaurant offered us its African and Middle Eastern music, some jazz pieces, and a few light classical selections, but no rock-and-roll, top of the pops, or blues, popular though blues music was among many of the brothers when they entered the NOI. After some instruction in the temple you learned to hear the blues for what they were—all those plaints about infidelity and adultery, about longing for another man's woman, about one lover going out the back door while another's coming in the front, about dark moods when love's gone wrong—and what they were was irrelevant to a Muslim lifestyle, besides being just plain depressing.

Sometimes, too, we would rent a film for Unity Night, usually a nature documentary produced by the National Geographic Society. Whether the film explored the silent majesty of the Himalayas or Africa's Great Rift Valley, the Sahara or Jacques Cousteau's world beneath the sea, Malcolm wanted us not only to discover the wonder and variety of all the realms in nature but also to appreciate their oneness as God's creation. All the films presented on Unity Night had educational or inspirational value. On the occasional Saturday at the temple we might show a Hollywood historical film about the Crusades, and only very rarely, for the exceptional big film like *Lawrence of Arabia*, which was Malcolm's favorite movie, did we actually go to commercial movie theaters.

For me, Tuesdays at the temple presented the week's biggest challenge and brought me the most personal reward. Tuesdays we had Malcolm's public speaking class. The class in fact had little to do with the techniques of preparing a speech or delivering a formal address, although one of the sisters who had taken a Dale Carnegie course in how to win friends and influence people did sometimes come in to give us a few pointers. Malcolm preferred to call it a public speaking class, however, because he didn't want any of his assistants' chests getting too swelled up by calling it his assistant minister class.

Malcolm demanded a lot of us. We had syllabuses, assignments, reports, book lists. We read the ancient history of peoples like the Chaldeans, Hittites, Egyptians, and Dravidians. We studied current events. Along with the daily *New York Times* and weekly news magazines like *Newsweek* and *Time* we read the London *Times* and, whenever possible, the *Peking Review*, and sometimes a newspaper from Indonesia, too. I set up a shortwave radio so we could pick up news on shortwave frequencies. We also studied philosophy, Chinese philosophy and Indian philosophy. We studied Sanskrit. We studied the Bible and the Koran. And we devoted many hours to geography. Malcolm wanted us to see exactly where on the map ancient tribes, kings, warriors, sages, prophets, and conquerors played out the events that molded their civilizations and became their history. He wanted us to see that the ancient Babylonians and Persians who built great cities and empires long before the Romans or Greeks originated not on the white man's continent that would one day be called Europe but in Asia Minor. Civilization, Malcolm wanted us to realize, was not born in the land of the supposedly superior white-skinned, blue-eyed, blond-haired devils as the white man would have African Americans believe. Geography proved the lie of the white man. Geography showed us, too, that all those so-called negroes who longed in their spirituals for the banks of the River Jordan didn't have to die to cross it, it's right there in the Middle East. Likewise, Egypt sits solidly in the northeast corner of Africa, where its pyramids and imposing monuments evidence its highly developed ancient civilization no matter how often Hollywood tries to make of Egypt some scary movie spook land.

Untruths had to be untold. Our minds had to be made new, said Malcolm. "Neither do men put new wine in old bottles," he said, quoting the Bible. We had to rid our minds of their misinformation, Malcolm explained, so that they could be prepared to receive the truth that would lead to our enlightenment. We had to be untaught before we could be taught, and once untaught, we ourselves could unteach others. That's why Malcolm initiated the public speaking class for his assistant ministers. A slave mentality impedes the development of a black Islamic consciousness, he told us. Until African Americans free themselves from European culture, myths, religion, history, and language, they will not take charge of their own destiny in America, he said. Our job, then, was to help our sisters and brothers correct four centuries of the white man's lies. First, though, we had to correct the lies inside ourselves.

At the first meeting of the class Malcolm listed some requirements: a notebook, a dictionary, a thesaurus, a book of synonyms and antonyms, an etymology text, a library card, and an open, willing mind. He expected us to study, and we studied. I mean, we really studied. We never wasted our leisure time on television, sports, movies, or parties in any case, but I was still working at Vanguard Records—this was in 1958—and finding it difficult to find the time to read and digest all the books that were piling up everywhere in my apartment. So I took a job for less pay but with more flexible hours as the superintendent of an apartment building on 141st Street. Most nights I'd study till after three in the morning. I'd usually fall asleep with my head in a book on top of the kitchen table; Malcolm was always telling us to study sitting straight up in a chair at the kitchen table. After a few hours' sleep I'd wake up, take out the garbage, mop floors, do odd jobs and repairs, and then clean myself up to go down to the temple. I'd socialize with the other assistants there or I'd talk with Malcolm, but mostly I'd study. I probably did more reading for Malcolm's public speaking class than most students do in four years of college; all of us did. I went out and bought an *Encyclopedia Britannica*, and still there were too many paths in Malcolm's woods to follow.

I always felt I had to listen closely to Malcolm whenever he spoke, but especially on Tuesdays in our class. He might be talking about astronomy one minute and bird migration the next, but he might not be really talking about either. One day, I remember, Malcolm was discussing the mystery of bird migration. Some theories state that birds follow landmarks, he said, while others hold that migratory birds follow the sun. Most birds, say many modern scientists, navigate by sky signs, particularly the stars, only that theory made Malcolm wonder about a bird like the Alaskan tern, which migrates over thirteen thousand miles but never flies at night. He also told us that many birds don't learn their migratory route; they are born with the knowledge inside them. He used an experiment with a particular species of bird that migrates every year from Germany to South Africa to illustrate this point. A group of ornithologists isolated one of these birds from its flock and took it to Spain. When the bird was released, it flew due north and east over the Swiss Alps into Germany, then turned and flew dead south to Africa. Although this bird itself had never before migrated anywhere by any route, it innately knew where to go, and went, perhaps by following the stars in the night sky's constellations or perhaps by some magnetic bearing. Once you've focused on a thing, said Malcolm, pointing up his meaning, if the thing you've focused on is right, you will be guided to your

destination even though you may not know how you are going to get there. Muslims, too, are guided to their destination
by the sun, the moon, and the stars. They are continually
being enlightened by the wisdom, literature, and scripture of
their prophets and philosophers, even when they don't know
it. Then Malcolm drew us an analogy. The prophets are like
the moon, he said, reflecting the light of the sun, which is
God, while we are like the ocean that reflects the light of the
moon. Our ocean is Islam, and our tides rise and fall at the
moon's bidding so that our waters may fill but not flood the
earth. Malcolm taught us that God's creation has much to
teach us about the nature of ourselves and our faith.

We studied the Bible extensively in our public speaking
class. Since an important part of an assistant minister's job
was converting the so-called negroes from the white man's
Christianity to Islam, we had to be familiar with the devil's
tool and with the ecclesiastical practices in his church. Actually, we had no argument with the scriptures themselves, and
certainly not with the teaching of the prophet Jesus. What
riled us was the use Christian preachers made of the Bible,
the way they twisted its truth to entrap and enslave the
minds of their black congregations. "Wheresoever the carcass is, there will the eagles be gathered together," Malcolm
would quote from a passage he had underlined in his time-
worn Bible, its pages dog-eared and the binding cracked.
Black people are this carcass, Malcolm would say, because
they have been kept in ignorance and their minds are dead.
The eagles, meanwhile, continue to rob and to strip our people bare, he'd say, and with unremitting white authority the
American eagle will continue cruelly and unjustly to govern
the downtrodden so-called negroes until they are awakened.
With the holy book that had been used to enslave them we
assistant ministers set out to awaken them.

We set out with more than a Bible. We also had the Koran,
two flags, and a stepladder, and we set up in front of a Chock
Full o' Nuts on the corner of 125th Street and Seventh Ave-

nue. This was our training ground. With the American flag to one side of us and the Islamic flag to the other—the star opposed by the crescent—we'd climb onto the stepladder and shout out to any passersby that they should stop a moment and listen, for we had a message from the Nation of Islam. Then we'd start our preaching. My first time out on the street corner that stepladder looked to me like the biggest hurdle I had confronted up to that point in my life, because I had been stuttering ever since I was a child. I could exhaust myself just getting out an *a* or a *the*. With Malcolm's help I had begun to overcome it. He had been teaching me to take a deep breath before I actually started speaking and that helped me avoid some of my stammering. He had been teaching me, too, to take my time with my thoughts, to concentrate totally on what I was saying, on the words I was forming, so that I would be able to speak in a loud, clear voice the truth that I had begun to know. He had been building my faith in my capabilities. I stepped up onto the ladder. I stood between the two flags with the Bible, the Koran, and my own words. I spoke out to a few people passing by. Others gathered. I spoke far from perfectly, but I met the challenge; I tried. I improved with time.

Malcolm sometimes stopped by the corner to watch his assistant ministers in action. On these occasions we would speak extra carefully so as not to lose our thoughts in our rhetoric or to pass on any misinformation. Malcolm took in every word and gesture, and he was not easily impressed. When I tried impressing him one day by repeating a statement he had made in our Tuesday class, he admonished me never to repeat anything I had heard from anybody, including him, until I myself had studied it. Only after I had confirmed its truth and made mine the knowledge that supported it, Malcolm advised, did I have the right to use it, to discuss it, or to answer questions regarding it. Usually, though, any comments Malcolm might have on our performance were received secondhand, from Captain Joseph. At least one of Captain Joseph's FOI lieutenants would wander up to the Chock Full o' Nuts during our street-corner preaching to observe and evaluate our delivery. He would then report back to Captain Joseph and the captain would pass on the lieutenant's remarks to Malcolm. The day did come that Captain Joseph told Malcolm that he had been getting really good reports on Brother Benjamin, that Brother Benjamin must be doing his homework, and Malcolm told the captain to tell Brother Benjamin to open up the next Wednesday meeting. The day would come, too, that Captain Joseph would be telling me that I'd be opening up for Malcolm at the General Civilization Nights on Fridays and finally, as Malcolm's first assistant minister, at our general public meetings on Sunday afternoons.

Malcolm left the subject of a street lecture or an opening speech in the temple up to the assistant minister himself. "Follow your mind," he would say. Single-minded, Brother Assistant Minister Curtis invariably lectured on the slave history of America. When he'd get to his description of whites castrating a black man, he'd picture it in such vivid detail that you'd think you yourself were actually witnessing it. On more than several occasions he got his street-corner crowd so wrought up that the precinct police telephoned Malcolm at the temple and urged him to pull Brother Curtis off his perch on the stepladder before he caused a riot. Malcolm, though, never censored Brother Curtis's subject matter. He trusted in his assistant's abilities, and his trust was not misplaced. One evening, in the middle of Brother Curtis's preaching, five police cars converged at the corner of 125th Street and Seventh Avenue. Their sirens wailing and tires screeching, they seemed to appear on cue but out of nowhere, and soon ten or twelve policemen were jumping into the street and pulling their guns. Frightened, the people in Brother Curtis's little crowd got ready to scatter. Brother Curtis, however, kept himself and them under control. "Don't you get excited," he told them as the policemen, their guns drawn, started running into the crowd. "Let them get excited," said Brother Curtis, keeping his hot indignation inside himself, and the people in his small crowd listened. They did not get excited, they did not disperse. Nor did any incident occur. So the police just plowed through them and burst into the Chock Full o' Nuts as if they had been called in to apprehend some suspicious character or other—with five squad cars. They came swaggering back out, with no suspicious character or other, and jumped back into their cars. They drove off noisily. Their ruse, like their tactics, had failed. They had wanted to break up our street-corner meeting, but Brother Curtis's presence of mind had bested them. He had learned Malcolm's lessons well; he had not allowed anger to blind his reason and he had not betrayed a trust.

There was one thing that Malcolm definitely did not like us doing, as I discovered one Sunday that I had been assigned to teach in Boston, and that was imitating Brother Minister. Malcolm had a way of pressing his forefinger against his temple while resting his thumb at the base of his chin; the gesture appears in many photographs where Malcolm is looking quietly inquisitive or contemplative. It was a gesture that I myself had adopted. So had Brother Louis Farrakhan. In the early days at Number Seven he and Malcolm had grown closer than most natural brothers. Malcolm had provided generously for Farrakhan and his family; he'd recommended him for the ministry at Boston Temple Number Eleven. Farrakhan admired Malcolm's personality more than he felt any debt to him, and he was a clever performer, formerly the leader of a calypso band, and a born entertainer with a gift for impressions. His forefinger on his temple and his thumb on his chin, he would get Malcolm's expressions exactly right, and then he'd mimic Malcolm's preaching style. I guess we all imitated Malcolm to some degree, because we all admired him so deeply. Malcolm, however, wanted us to be ourselves and evolve a preaching style of our own. So that Sunday morning, after we had said our good-byes and I was practically out the door on my way to Boston, Malcolm stopped me dead. "And tell Minister Louis to stop imitating me," he said, and I knew by his look the message was meant as much for me as for the minister of Number Eleven.

Once I started preaching I started traveling from time to time, to teach at the temples in Boston and Philadelphia, or in Washington, where I was acting minister for a while, and in Newark, New Haven, Providence. With Malcolm and the other assistant ministers I helped set up temples in Brooklyn and Queens, and I spent a lot of time commuting to Bridgeport, Connecticut. The success of our New Haven temple aroused the interest of some people in Bridgeport, so I began visiting with them in their homes each week and each week I'd be visiting with three or four more. After the teaching tea and cake or some sandwiches would be served; we'd socialize. We'd also take a collection because all NOI temples, even the baby temples, as the house meeting groups were called, were expected to support themselves. Self-supporting, the baby gradually grew. Eventually it outgrew the private living rooms of our brothers and sisters in Bridgeport and we rented a public space. In the same way, in 1930, some thirty years before, the first Muslim temple had been founded in Detroit by W.D. Fard.

Wherever I traveled and taught, however, in none of the temples I visited during my seven years as Malcolm's assistant minister, or any time since, not in Chicago or Detroit or on the West Coast, did I attend any convention, rally, debate, or lecture that could quite compare with the public speaking class taught by our brother teacher Malcolm every Tuesday inside Temple Number Seven.

Remembering Malcolm

In July 1959, on the news show *News Beat*, WDNT-TV aired "The Hate That Hate Produced." The five-part report by Mike Wallace featured Malcolm X, among others, and for the first time brought the black Muslim movement to the attention of the general American public. That telecast also established Malcolm X as the spokesman for Elijah Muhammad and the NOI with the news media.

In the months that followed and throughout the early sixties the words of Malcolm X were constantly being quoted in the daily press. His voice was frequently heard in radio interviews, and on television screens across the nation his face was seen repeatedly on the evening news. Fiery, forceful, in indignation, rage, anger, or scorn, Malcolm X was telling America that white people were the devil, that their conscienceless sins were soon to be punished by the wrath of Allah, that their cities would burn, that their children were cursed. White America was also learning that for Malcolm X "coffee with a [Georgia] cracker" in no way compensated blacks for the racist oppression they had been suffering for four hundred years. He was making it clear that the black Muslims stood firmly opposed to integration, and until their separatist goals were achieved, they demanded power over their own communities as well as their own destiny. Malcolm X also spoke eloquently of a people's pride and worth and dignity. What Malcolm X said sold the news, and the news sold Malcolm X. The image became familiar: the balled fist or pointed finger, the raised arm, the jaw militantly clenched, the grimace, the snarl. The stance, however, remained fierce, and in the face of Malcolm's inflammatory black nationalist rhetoric all indifference fled.

To many Americans, black as well as white, "the militant major-domo of the black Muslims," as *Playboy* magazine captioned him in 1963, harbingered only violence. Others saw him as an intolerant zealot mongering the very kind of racist hatred that he himself condemned in the ubiquitous white devil. Some found hope in the vision of the fearlessly outspoken Malcolm X, and in the promise of revolution the possibility of a world more equitable and a society more just.

The Malcolm that Benjamin Karim admired so deeply and observed daily at Temple Number Seven is not readily circumscribed by one idea or one emotion. Nor is he easily defined. He is remembered.

* * *

Whatever the media may have led many people to believe, the ministry at Temple Number Seven was not dedicated to brainwashing blacks with the study of slave history in order to teach them to hate whites any more than Malcolm was some crazy, wild-eyed extremist. Temple Number Seven was not a racist institution. It was an institution of learning. Malcolm had a mission, the education of blacks who had been living in the cave of ignorance for four hundred years, and he made that mission ours as well. He presented it to the assistant ministers like this: If you take a man who has been living in a cave for four hundred years and all at once you introduce him to daylight, the sudden exposure to the open sky full of sunshine could blind the caveman or drive him mad. Covering his eyes with his hands, in pain, he would retreat back into the darkness he thought was his protection. He would never want to see daylight again. So we had to bring light beam by beam into the cave of our lost-found sisters and brothers. Ray by ray we had to illuminate their intellectual darkness, because for most of us enlightenment comes gradually, through the process of learning, not suddenly like an apocalypse. By degrees we had to redeem them from their ignorance.

What Malcolm hated most was ignorance. Malcolm hated ignorance more than he hated the white men who had driven the so-called negroes into the cave and into enslavement. Malcolm felt, though, that black people had to bear some of the blame for their own unenlightenment. You can blame a person for knocking you down, Malcolm often said, but you can't blame that person if you refuse to get back up. Nor could we blame the white man that for four hundred years we ourselves had failed even to try to find a way out of the cave. However much slave history taught us about the injustice and misery we as a people had suffered, it did not excuse us from assuming responsibility for ourselves and each other by altering its course. Our hopes of doing that, for Malcolm, lay in education. His hope sometimes dimmed. "How many dictionaries and reference books do you suppose we would collect if we went through a black housing project in New York?" he lamented once. "Enough to fill a car trunk or van?" he asked. "Or maybe a suitcase?" We can't blame the white man, he said, for the dictionaries black children don't have. Poverty, said Malcolm, provides no excuse for ignorance any more than history does. Ignorance breeds poverty, he said, it's not the other way around.

The human mind, then, was Malcolm's battleground. Armed with words, ideas, and common sense, he fought the enemy ignorance. He did not preach violence, he preached consciousness. (Malcolm did not tolerate violence, in fact. At public rallies and outdoor meetings the FOI, along with the police, kept security tight. We allowed no beer or alcohol; we took every measure to prevent any fights from breaking out. Any open arguments in the audience were settled by Malcolm himself, usually with a few words spoken very politely, like, "Brother, you're not being yourself today." Of course, some people might be stirred toward violence by the force of Malcolm's words, but they would all leave the premises quietly, thoughtfully, and not even a chewing-gum wrapper would be left on the ground behind them.) Thought was what Malcolm wanted to provoke. He wanted to awaken the minds of black people into a consciousness of their condition so that they could begin actively to eliminate the gross inequities that divided them from the rest of the population, most of it also ignorant, in America's racist society. Malcolm wanted black people to work, because he believed that work raised self-esteem and that you had to be able to support yourself before you could support Islam. He wanted black people to study. He wanted them to care for and educate their children in the ways of Islam, for in their children's children and in their grandchildren's children lay the future of the Nation. He wanted black people to take pride in themselves, not only in the color of their skin and texture of their hair but also in the quality of their intelligence, and he wanted them to better themselves. He also wanted them to be aware that certain whites, those in positions of power and authority, would be out there as they had always been, at least for four centuries, trying to play bad games with their brains.

As a minister in the Nation of Islam, Malcolm wanted American blacks to have both their own religion and their own nation. That's why we went "fishing." We were fishing when we were preaching on our stepladder outside Chock Full o' Nuts. We often went fishing outside churches, too, for Christians. Once we had gotten their attention it was easy to rouse their curiosity because everyone had at least heard of Malcolm X. If we also got them interested in the NOI message to brothers and sisters lost in the wilderness, we would go round and pick them up at their houses later that day or the next week to take them to the Sunday meeting at the temple. We recruited hundreds of Christians into the NOI that way.

We fished the streets as well, for junkies, pushers, winos, gamblers, and in the temple we'd work together with Malcolm to rid them of their addictions, to reform them.

In his work with the brothers off the street Malcolm had sometimes unbelievable success, Gladstone being one I'll never forget. I fished in Gladstone. When I brought him to the temple to hear Malcolm, he had been shooting so much heroin into his veins that the punctures, running like sores up and down the length of his arm, never had a chance to heal. Nonetheless, in two weeks Gladstone was ready to write his letter to Chicago. More surprisingly, though, with the aid of Malcolm's powers of persuasion, he had also kicked his habit. I couldn't believe it; it seemed to me that in Gladstone's case Malcolm had performed something like a miracle. The New York police detective who dropped a plain white envelope containing a packet of heroin for Gladstone at a candy store on Lenox Avenue couldn't believe it either. Gladstone did pick up the plain white envelope from the owner of the candy store, but he never opened it. In the eight years I knew him, to my knowledge, Gladstone never used drugs again.

Malcolm's powers of persuasion did not entirely succeed with Fidel Castro. In September 1960, when Castro came to New York to speak at the United Nations, the press got word from his midtown hotel that along with his entourage Castro was traveling with live chickens, to be sure he'd have untainted poultry, and evidently he'd had their necks wrung in his hotel room. Blood was splattered, and feathers were strewn, everywhere, on the walls, carpet, bedspreads, chairs. The press was having a field day. So Malcolm sent word to Castro that he should move uptown to the Hotel Theresa. An FOI brother, Luqman, who was working with the Cubans on security at the hotel, was informed by a Cuban official that Castro would like to meet with Malcolm. Luqman rushed down to the temple restaurant with Castro's request, which I relayed to Malcolm. The three of us got into

Malcolm's dark blue Oldsmobile and drove up to the Theresa on 125th Street, but only Malcolm went up to Castro's room. After some while, when he came back down, Malcolm said the meeting had been congenial, but he offered no details. Later he revealed that he had tried to do a little fishing that afternoon. He'd tried to get Castro to become a Muslim, he said, and Castro hadn't said no. He hadn't said yes, either.

Castro or Gladstone, waitresses and bodyguards and assistant ministers, longtime Muslims or any one of hundreds of Christians, anyone who attended to Malcolm shared in the resources of his remarkable mind. At the temple he continually inspired us with his knowledge, thought, judgment, and philosophy. With no tutor to guide him, from the Upanishads to Karl Marx, he had traveled intellectual worlds as far-flung as the Athens of Socrates and the ancient China of Lao Tzu, worlds culturally totally alien to his own, and he had conquered them. Against all odds he had become an intellectual phenomenon. No other American of color, it seemed to us, could rival the diversity of Malcolm's intellect, his encyclopedic mind, the startling logic, his swift wit and intelligence. Not Booker T. Washington, who founded the Tuskegee Institute in Alabama in 1881, or George Washington Carver, who derived three hundred products from the peanut in his agricultural experiments there; not the great orator and abolitionist Frederick Douglass or the educator W.E.B. Du Bois. We had known no one quite like Malcolm. Nor did we know quite what to make of him. Nor did anyone.

For most people in mainstream American society, Malcolm was like his X. An unknown. And that caused them anxiety, fear, and uncertainty. The government didn't know how to deal with him, except to have the FBI keep a file on him. The press photographed and quoted him, then tried to make the whole man fit the shallow mold it made of him. Professors at Harvard tried to match wits with him, as did the civil rights leaders who dared to enter into public debate with him.

What was certain, as everyone who encountered him soon discovered, was that the mind behind the image was irrepressible. Malcolm X never lacked an answer or wanted for a comeback. He seemed to know something about everything, and he spoke with authority on most things. How do you measure the genius? How do you fathom the intelligence? I worked under Malcolm's instruction at Temple Number Seven. I studied with him for seven years. I traveled with him. At meetings and rallies I opened up for him. I listened to him. The parts of the man that I knew for eight years don't make up the whole, however. I can't put a circle around the X and say, "This is the man, this is the real Malcolm." I can only say what I remember of the man I knew.

I knew him as Brother Minister or Brother Minister Malcolm, and everyone knew whom you meant by "the Minister." No one in the temple, though, ever called him Malcolm or Malcolm X. *Minister:* Malcolm wrote it on the blackboard. *"Minister,"* he said, "from the Latin word for servant; an agent, pastor, officer, ambassador." He explained that a minister is not just a servant of God or an agent between God and His people. Relating *minister* to words like *administer* and *ministrate,* he said a minister also manages, protects, supervises, and dispenses judgments as well as moral medicine. Brother Minister Malcolm was our counselor, healer, judge, instructor, teacher, and peacemaker. And our listener, because you can't minister if you're not a listener.

Malcolm listened intently. Whether he was following the opening argument in a debate or an assistant minister's lecture or the ins and outs of a Muslim couple's marital problems, he gave the speaker his full attention. Malcolm placed no less importance on listening than he did on speaking. He considered it an art, and he brought to it the same high level of skill and technique that he brought to his oratory. He taught us, the assistant ministers, that to teach we had to learn but to learn we had to listen. We had to listen as much with our minds as with our ears and concentrate on a speaker's thoughts as well as the words. To listen effectively required discrimination and objectivity, Malcolm said. He taught us not to allow our own feelings and prejudices to color our perceptions so that we could draw valid conclusions and make sound judgments from what we heard. We learned to listen for key words that developed a line of argument. We learned to pay attention to emphasis and to a speaker's inflections, which might reveal more to us than the words meant in themselves. Again, Malcolm set us a perfect example. He treated us the way he treated all speakers, the way he himself would want to be treated: with respect, sensitivity, interest, and close attention.

Inside the temple Minister Malcolm offered a sympathetic and attentive ear to any brothers or sisters experiencing emotional crises or domestic difficulties. Malcolm felt his responsibility to the lost-found brothers and sisters had only begun with their entry into the temple, as they themselves had only just begun their personal battles against four centuries of ignorance. If his words had wooed them into the Nation, then his words had to continue to support them in their commitment to the Muslim lifestyle and Islamic moral principles. When Malcolm counseled them, he patiently strove to get to the root of the problem so that he could focus on its cause and not deal merely with effects. Counseling occurred in private only at the request of the brother or sister seeking advice. It more commonly took place before the general body, after a regular meeting, because other brothers and sisters in similar circumstances might benefit from the discussion and from Malcolm's advice. In one instance that I recall Malcolm probably saved more than one shaky marriage and no doubt solved communication problems in dozens of others in the matter of an hour.

Malcolm spoke about corn. The problem, though, appeared to be pork, or pork bacon, which the non-Muslim wife of an FOI brother frequently cooked and ate. The young woman regularly attended temple meetings and for the most part accepted the Muslim ways, but despite Malcolm's vehement lectures on the swine and her husband's own exhortations, she had failed to rid her diet and the refrigerator of bacon. The brother was preparing to sue for divorce. The offense to the brother being pork, everyone was of course expecting Malcolm to launch into a tirade condemning the woman to perdition for eating the unclean meat of the pig. But he didn't. Instead he pointed out that the young woman had not yet entered into the Nation of Islam and was therefore not yet subject to its dietary laws. Then he compared the woman and her husband to two grains of corn. Both grains were planted in the earth at the same time, as he related it, and one quickly sprouted, its tender roots finding water in the soil while its young shoot climbed toward the sun. Its stalk grew tall and strong. The other grain of corn lagged far behind. Its stem was frail when it broke through the ground. It wanted light, but uprooted it would surely die. In its own time, at its own pace, the delicate shoot found its way to the sun and it, too, grew to be strong.

We can find wisdom in the ways of nature, Malcolm explained. We have to give people time to come to their enlightenment as they can, he said. Understanding may come slowly, but it must come naturally. We cannot simply transplant the frail believers among us in foreign soil and expect them to grow. Nor can we condemn them for what we cannot force them to be. We all come to our choices differently, said Malcolm. That night, as soon as the young woman and her husband got home, she went directly into the kitchen and opened the refrigerator. She threw the bacon into the garbage. Brother Minister Malcolm had shown the Muslim brother that neither condemnation nor force could solve his problem. He had shown the young wife that enlightenment lay in her hands, that she had a choice. Malcolm of course was not just speaking to the two of them any more than he was talking corn or pork. He was teaching all six hundred of us in the temple congregation the values of discretion, patience, and reason in all our human relationships.

Reason, discretion, and patience never failed Malcolm in his ministry at Number Seven. Nor did a stroke of sheer inspiration when he needed it. One day when a sister came into the temple restaurant looking for Malcolm, and looking frantic, he needed it. The woman's husband, a brother at the temple, had spooked out. ("Don't get so wrapped up in God that you lose sight of the world," Malcolm used to tell us, "and don't get so wrapped up in the world you lose sight of God; you have to maintain a balance." When you spooked out, you had definitely lost the balance.)

Distraught, the woman told us that about six weeks earlier her husband had begun to take Bible study more seriously so he could more readily follow Malcolm's teachings from the holy scriptures. Four weeks ago, she said, he was taking it so seriously that he was studying the Bible every spare minute of every day and he had become so absorbed in the New Testament that he'd begun talking aloud to Jesus. Then he'd started seeing Jesus. Raising her eyes to heaven and clasping her face between her hands, she shook her head in disbelief and related that Jesus had begun giving her husband orders, or so our spooked-out brother believed. First Jesus had told him to throw out all the books in the house, except for the Bible. So he had emptied the bookshelves and the magazine rack, and one by one he had tossed every single magazine and book, including the sister's cookbooks, out the back window into the yard. Then Jesus had told the brother to turn the face of the television to the wall. He did, and in the evenings his poor wife was reduced to sitting in their living room without a book and staring at the backside of a television set while her husband read his Bible and talked with Jesus. Finally, just a few days before, our deluded brother had been told by Jesus to quit his job, and now they were conversing full time. The sister confessed that shame had kept her from seeking out Malcolm sooner, but she had reached the point that she didn't know where to turn or what to do, particularly since Muslims as a rule did not consult psychiatrists.

All the while the woman had been speaking her unfortunate story Malcolm had been listening to her closely, without interrupting. He had a way of holding his head back and furrowing his brow that showed she had captured his attention, and concern, but he didn't look upset or become excited. He turned to me and Brother Louis 2X and said, "You go and get that brother and take him somewhere to watch cartoons."

I loved cartoons, Brother Louis 2X loved cartoons. We were happy to carry out Minister Malcolm's instructions. Exactly why we were taking a brother who had spooked out on Jesus to watch cartoons was not, however, clear to us. In Times Square we found one of those New York movie houses that used to show cartoons all day Saturdays, and from late in the morning though the entire afternoon, with our freaky brother sitting between us, Louis 2X and I kept one eye on him and the other on Looney Tunes. Bugs Bunny, Daffy Duck, Porky Pig, Woody Woodpecker, one after the other they chomped, quacked, spluttered, and ha-ha-ha-ha-haed their way through several hours of animated mishap and catastrophe before our brother stirred. For three hours or more he had been staring solemnly at the screen without even a titter, but once he started laughing, quietly at first, he didn't stop, and soon he was really cracking up, so Brother Louis 2X and I didn't know if he was spooking out again or simply enjoying a tomcat's introduction to electric shock by a mouse named Jerry. We left at the end of the afternoon. We had walked about half a block when our brother, seemingly less disturbed than he had been five or six hours earlier, stopped. He looked at the two of us, me and Louis, on either side of him. "You know," he said, "I must have really frightened my wife." That's all he said, but you could tell that he was cured. Brother Louis 2X and I knew then why

Malcolm had asked us to take the brother who spoke to Jesus out somewhere to watch cartoons. Why it worked I'm still not sure.

One thing sure, Malcolm possessed inventiveness. Focusing wholly on any problem that any of us at the temple presented to him, he came quickly to his insight. Along with it usually came a unique solution or uniquely stated advice, and often humor, too. I remember one brother who had been cost a considerable strain financially as well as emotionally by a family emergency. He sought out the minister's counsel at the temple restaurant. Malcolm listened attentively to the brother's story, then replied that for all of us life held the unexpected and we often met it unprepared. The observation came with a kind of fairy tale.

In olden times, the tale began, a king ruled the land with his beautiful, dark-skinned daughter by his side. His long dead queen had long been his only grief, but he had lately begun to regret that he had produced no male heir. Before he died he wished to know a son, and so he decided to offer his beautiful, dark-eyed daughter in marriage to any man whose brave deeds could claim her hand. Her suitor would first have to swim hazardous river rapids to the east of the castle, then slice a path through the thicket and wild meadow that surrounded it, then cross the castle moat, its depths alive with crocodiles, then scale the castle walls and finally, from the parapets, do battle with a fire-breathing dragon.

Many tried, many failed.

One day a handsome, well-proportioned youth of some wit but little ambition found himself among another dozen suitors who had gathered, and with second thoughts paused, at the banks of the angry, swollen river. Suddenly, the youth found himself in the river. Sinewy, he fought the current, and with skills till then untested he skirted rocks and rapids. On the far side he emerged tired, sore, and badly bruised. His clothes were torn. His clothes were shredded by the time he had cut a path with his sword through the thicket's thorny underbrush. As he stumbled into the open meadow a terrible hum pierced his ears, and the swarms of buzzing insects also bit. Scratched, chafed, bitten, bruised, he dove for relief into the cool, quiet water of the moat, and never learned it harbored crocodiles. He scaled the castle wall. He faced a fire-breathing dragon. Its flame singed the luster in his black, curly hair and in clouds of smoke he gasped for air. He thrust and he parried, and though he failed to slay the dragon, he didn't fail escaping it. And he kissed the hand of the king's beautiful, dark-haired daughter.

"The hand you have kissed is yours," the king informed him, "and whatever else in all my kingdom you desire."

"There is nothing in your kingdom I desire," replied the exhausted, nearly naked, singed, and battered youth, "not even the hand of your beautiful daughter."

The king was puzzled. "Is there nothing then that you want?" the king inquired.

"The only thing I want," answered the youth, "is the name of the sucker who pushed me into that river."

As much as a lifetime teaches us that we have to expect the unexpected we are rarely fully prepared for it. It tests our mettle and intellect, it taxes our strength, it calls upon our emotional reserves. Malcolm helped the man in the family emergency to learn to persevere. Survival, he taught all of us in the restaurant that day, requires discipline, spiritual fiber, all your wits, and resourcefulness. He followed the story of the unintentional suitor with an analogy. He compared life to a hammer and human beings to metal and glass. A hammer that beats upon metal can forge it into a bowl or tool or some other useful instrument, he said, but a hammer that beats upon glass shatters it into thousands of fragments and splinters. A lifetime hammers what we are made of into what we are.

Being an assistant minister assigned to the temple in Bridgeport, I, too, was often presented with problems or asked for advice by brothers and sisters. I didn't always have the answers. At one of our house meetings in Bridgeport a brother asked me what was the strongest urge in a human being. I told him the sex urge, the urge to reproduce yourself, because for married couples in the NOI the act of sex is also an act of creation and propagation by which you not only continue your family line but also build the Muslim nation. Later, back in New York, I consulted with Malcolm on my reply. He disagreed. He said that the strongest human urge was hunger. Take a man's food away from him for a week or even just a three-day fast, Malcolm said to illustrate, then place the most beautiful woman you can find to one side of him and to the other a plate of broiled lamb chops with mashed potatoes, fresh peas, a tossed green salad, some hot rolls and butter, and see which one he will sample first. You could strip the woman naked, Malcolm wagered, and the man would still choose the food first. Hunger is the more basic drive, Malcolm said, because a person can live without sex but not without nourishment.

Malcolm's deeds spoke to us as eloquently as his words, especially on the topic of hunger. One night Malcolm was driving the four of us—me, him, Brother Louis 2X, and Captain Joseph—up to Bridgeport for a meeting. When Malcolm brought his Oldsmobile to a stop at a traffic light on Seventh Avenue, a winehead looking for a handout came up to the driver's side of the car and asked Malcolm, Mr. X he called him, for fifty cents. He was hungry, he said, and wanted to get himself a bowl of bean soup. Fifty cents in those days would have bought the old man a big, wide bowl of bean soup and a healthy piece of corn bread to go with it. Or a bottle of cheap wine. In either case, and very probably the latter, Malcolm gave the man the money. So we continued along Seventh Avenue, all of us sitting in the car and saying nothing. Three of us, though, were no doubt thinking that we were supposed to be pulling fish like that old winehead into the temple; we were supposed to be scaling them of their bad habits and cleaning them up, leading them out of their ignorance, not giving them fifty cents to buy more alcohol. We had driven maybe twenty blocks farther in our weighty silence when Malcolm said abruptly, "I know what you're thinking."

"No, you don't, Brother Minister," I replied. "But you know you gave yourself away right then. Because we're not thinking things."

"Yes, you are," Malcolm returned. "You're thinking that I don't know if that old man is going to buy a bottle of wine or if he's going to buy himself some food. You know why I gave him fifty cents? I gave him fifty cents because he told me he was hungry. I can't say that he was or wasn't hungry, because I'm not him, but I can tell you that had I not given him the money, it would have bothered my mind that he might have been depending on my fifty cents to get something to eat. It would have bothered me because I can afford the fifty cents to feed him." Then Malcolm started talking about charity. The female ant, he told us, will regurgitate her food to feed another ant. Nature sends flying insects into the air to provide nourishment for birds on the wing, he said. Rain falls upon the earth, and in the soil its water brings minerals to the roots of plants. Out of one grain of corn grows a stalk that will bear an exceptionally generous seven full ears. Nature everywhere evidences God's bountiful charity, Malcolm showed us all the way to Bridgeport. Charity is not judging your brother, said Malcolm, it's neither believing nor disbelieving an old man who speaks of hunger. Charity is taking advantage of the opportunity to be able to feed him, an opportunity, he added, that he himself would never miss.

Charity lay at the heart of Malcolm's ministry. To the sisters and brothers in the temple Malcolm gave unremittingly and generously of his time, energy, care, and spirit. He gave us his ear, he shared with us his wisdom. He met our needs willingly. Whatever Malcolm could afford to give he gave, and many times what he couldn't really afford to give he gave. On one occasion Malcolm was approached in the temple by a sister who had fallen into such bad financial straits that she was finding it continually more difficult to feed her two little children. Despite her desperation she had found it difficult, too, to swallow her pride and call upon the minister for help, for a loan, but she no longer knew where to turn, she said. Malcolm asked what she needed. Thirty-five or forty dollars, she said, and with no hesitation Malcolm reached into his pocket and gave her the thirty-five to forty dollars that was in it. He told the temple secretary to make a note of it, but that didn't mean anything. Malcolm simply gave the despairing woman what she needed because at that moment she needed it more than he.

Minister Malcolm did not allow the financial demands of his own family—a wife and three children, by 1962—on his NOI salary of $175 a week stand in the way of his charity. (Assistant ministers received no money at all from the NOI; I had my job as a building superintendent, and at rallies and public meetings I sold Islamic literature that I imported from England and Pakistan.) All the money Malcolm raised with his oratory at NOI rallies all over the country—millions, I'd estimate—of course went directly to the national headquarters in Chicago. More than any other NOI minister's addresses or any NOI official's funding efforts, Malcolm's oratory supplied the capital for the NOI leadership's various businesses and properties like the sixteen hundred acres of orchard and farmland in Indiana, the mansion in Chicago, and the Arizona real estate. Also, the thirty or forty thousand dollars Malcolm raised for a new Muslim temple in New York first went to Chicago (it never came back). Even the money Malcolm earned in speaker's fees for his lectures at universities and colleges during the early sixties had to be passed on to national headquarters because Malcolm was speaking as a representative of the NOI. Inside the temple or out Malcolm did what he did not for personal reward or gain but for the betterment of his brothers and sisters. Minister

Malcolm had a mission, and with his deeds and words he brought light to our ignorance. What he did he had to do.

He spoke. In the temple he taught, in public he preached. Malcolm might be lecturing from the temple platform or addressing students in a college auditorium or opening a rally in a public arena, but he would always prepare himself in the same way. Once he had determined where he wanted his words and ideas to take him, he would search the library in his mind as well as the bookshelves in his study, which was in the attic of his home in Queens, for the information that would help him accomplish his objective. As he selected each piece of information pertinent to his premises he would write down a cue to it on a three-by-five index card. Suppose, for instance, he was lecturing on the liberation of the so-called negro. And say he had decided to underscore the point that Mr. Muhammad was leading the lost-founds out of the North American wilderness into their own nation by comparing the Messenger to Moses leading the children of Israel out of Egypt. For his cue Malcolm would simply write the word *Moses* on the card. At the same time he was accumulating his cue cards he was continually arranging and rearranging them until he settled finally upon the pattern for his thoughts. With the cards he would then perhaps rehearse his arguments in his mind. By the time Malcolm stepped up to the podium he probably didn't need his three-by-five cue cards at all. Before he would begin to speak, though, he would riffle through them one more time, as if he was reconsidering their arrangement. What he was really doing was dealing with his nerves and tension, for a few seconds settling himself, before beginning his delivery.

Malcolm had tremendous presence when he spoke, and he brought a stirring energy to his words. His mind worked like fire, in part because Malcolm never ate before a lecture. He didn't want digestion calling blood to his stomach when he needed it to carry oxygen to his brain, so he could think more efficiently. The same could not always be said for some

of the Christians we fished into the temple on a Sunday afternoon. They would have just finished eating a big noontime
meal after their Sunday morning church service when we'd
pick them up for our two o'clock meeting. For all the power
of spirit and force of reason in Malcolm's delivery, they'd be
sitting there with their chins in their hands, their heads
propped up but their eyelids drooping, and one by one
they'd start nodding off. One Sunday I especially remember,
Malcolm suddenly roared out, "What we should do here in
Harlem is get us some matches and burn all these Christian
churches down!" That awoke them sure enough. Not that
Malcolm would ever have burnt any church down. He merely
wanted to shock his dozing Christians into attention, and he
succeeded.

At meetings, rallies, forums, debates, all the while Malcolm was commanding the podium, no matter how absorbed
by the force of his own words he might appear to be, he
never lost contact with his audience. He was watchful, and
even when he was speaking he was, in a sense, listening. He
listened of course to the comments and questions that came
from the audience. He listened, too, for appreciative laughter as well as for groans or sighs. He heard the occasional
gibe or outburst, and he enjoyed the applause. More subtly,
he was also listening to what wasn't being spoken or really
being heard, to what you might call the pulse of the audience. Malcolm's intuitive ear kept him attuned to the people
in his audience—people from the Harlem business community, church people, Muslims, reporters who covered his career and would be quoting him, intellectuals, activists,
political figures who took their cues from Malcolm but never
outwardly supported him—and it kept him attuned to the
feeling that he himself had created in them as an audience.
With every inner sense he listened as he spoke, and he responded. He responded to hope or anger or outrage. He responded to the cry of his people. Throughout his ministry he

sought to cure the social ills that afflicted twenty-two million African Americans.

By the thousands people responded to Malcolm. At outdoor rallies in Harlem we would draw huge crowds by beating on drums you could hear, depending on the weather, ten, twelve, or twenty city blocks away. In droves the people would gather, and when Malcolm took the microphone they would all fall silent, thousands of them. I have seen Malcolm hold a crowd like that spellbound, even in the rain. Their concentration so intense, forgetting even to blink until their eyes went dry, and then looking as if they were awakening from a trance, they stood there in the rain, many of them without umbrellas, listening to Malcolm X. It seemed that nothing could dampen the fire in Malcolm's words. After a rally Malcolm would leave the public platform or stage and head for his waiting car. We'd drive him away. Sitting back, unwinding, he'd begin to slip back into his private self, and he would be very hungry.

Malcolm was equally compelling with his audiences on university and college campuses, where he always had more than a few things to teach the faculty as well as the student body. In one of his college lectures that I particularly remember, no doubt because of a confused or simply hostile white student in the audience, Malcolm set out to correct some of the lies being taught in American schools about the history of slavery in the United States. African slaves, said Malcolm, had laid the economic foundation of America during the colonial period and had borne the burden of its agrarian development throughout the nineteenth century. Generations of African Americans, however, had yet to receive one cent in compensation for their labor. The Emancipation Proclamation won for black people only empty promises, Malcolm asserted. He pointed out that the government that was promising former slaves freedom and the economic opportunity of forty acres and a mule was at the same time annihilating Native Americans as the nation expanded west. Opportunity swiftly declined into sharecropping in the South and drudgery in the industrial North. The twentieth century did nothing to rectify the injustices of the past, said Malcolm. Instead, law officers were turning water cannons and attack dogs on the defenseless women and children, students, and unarmed black men who were demonstrating for their civil rights. If modern America did not reverse its inequitable policies and alter its historical course, Malcolm concluded, the country would destroy itself from within and its international power would shrink into insignificance. The past had its price, he said. By the end of his lecture Malcolm had the students in his predominantly white audience almost in awe, with one exception.

After the lecture, when Malcolm offered to answer any questions from the audience, this hulking white student in a baseball cap stood up in the front of the balcony. "Mr. X," he said, and in his voice you could hear a belligerence, "you're just like Adolf Hitler!" I have no idea where this remark came from, considering the point of Malcolm's lecture. Nor had Malcolm been talking about white devils or genetic determinance or Armageddon and the black Muslim victory; Malcolm didn't preach NOI doctrine in his college lectures. "You're talking the same stuff Adolf Hitler talked," the student accused Malcolm.

Malcolm did not point out the irrelevance of the student's comment to the lecture. He replied that in order to develop the racist theories that would lead first to the persecution and later to the mass extermination of millions of Jews, Hitler had studied American history. Malcolm then expanded on the horrors of racism both in Hitler's Germany and in the United States, a nation that made an institution of slavery. He spoke vehemently of the atrocities suffered by slaves who were meticulously skinned alive or beheaded, their heads then posted on stakes, or castrated or burnt alive in stadiums as a public spectacle. As Malcolm spoke the student in the baseball cap slid down into his seat. He had pulled the beak of the cap down over his face, and then the cap disappeared. The student slinked out of the auditorium. Malcolm finished to thunderous applause. Afterward the students gathered around him like bees around honey in August. They asked him questions about their studies, they sought his advice on term-paper topics, they requested his autograph. Malcolm answered and counseled and obliged.

One of Malcolm's lectures on slave history at a New England college so upset a young woman at the school that she followed Malcolm back to New York. Petite, and pretty, with sandy hair and pale skin, she was almost crying when she arrived at the temple restaurant. She spotted Malcolm immediately; he was having a cup of coffee with me, Brother Louis 2X, and Captain Joseph. She came over to the table, and in a white southern accent she asked Malcolm if he truly didn't believe there were any good white people. Malcolm replied that he didn't believe in people's words, only their deeds. She then asked him what she could do. Nothing, Malcolm informed her, and suggested that if she had learned anything that day, she might go back and try teaching it to her own people. He was very blunt with her. Her eyes were filling with tears when she left. I felt sorry for her.

I think Malcolm would have responded differently to the young woman if Captain Joseph, Louis 2X, and I had not been present. We had after all been taught by the temple that all white people were devils, so Malcolm had to maintain a hard NOI exterior and not show a young white woman kindness or concern. After she had gone, the conversation took a heavy turn and Malcolm seemed almost to be lamenting his responses to the college girl without once referring to her. On another occasion many months later Malcolm said to me, in reference to the NOI position on white devils, "When you realize that you're wrong, admit it. Even if it is against yourself, when you know for sure you're wrong, admit it. Regardless of the consequences, admit the truth and apologize." I think Malcolm would have liked to have had the chance to apologize to the young woman who followed him from her college in New England to a Muslim restaurant in New York.

Throughout the early sixties Malcolm welcomed every opportunity to speak to college students. He felt that he could reach young undergraduates by dealing with issues of race and history in an intellectual, reasoned way. He found them ready to listen and eager to hear what he had to say. He spoke to them as a teacher. He invited them to open their minds, to think, to call upon their knowledge and logic in order to see the fallacies of America's past and to imagine its future possibilities. He appealed to their sense of justice. He sometimes frightened their administrators, particularly at New York City's municipal colleges. The Queens College administration barred Malcolm from speaking there in 1961. Student demonstrations failed to reverse the decision, but a month or so later the dean of City College submitted to student pressure and allowed a left-wing campus organization to invite the controversial, perhaps dangerous Malcolm X to speak at an assembly there. Malcolm was dangerous. He was dangerous like an idea is dangerous.

National officials in the NOI, meanwhile, had also begun to read danger in Malcolm's activity as a lecturer on college campuses like those of Boston University, Cornell, and Harvard. They were complaining to Mr. Muhammad that Malcolm was spending too much time outside the temple, that he wasn't really representing the NOI because he wasn't teaching Armageddon and the doom of the white devil in lakes burning with eternal fire. In fact, they pointed out, he was speaking for the most part *to* the white devil. They did, however, welcome his speaker's fees. They were also saying that Malcolm's often highly publicized activities attracted too much attention from the media, which exaggerated his role as a Muslim minister in the Nation and lent him undue authority as an NOI spokesman. Malcolm's danger to the NOI leaders lay not only in his growing popularity with the press and a non-Muslim public but also in the influence he might usurp from them with Elijah Muhammad. They felt threatened. They were jealous.

Because of his sensitivity to the biases of power in Chicago, Malcolm became increasingly uncomfortable with his public profile. He didn't like wearing Joseph's many-colored coat. That was also why he waited for years to trade in his old, beat-up Chevrolet. The car was practically falling apart on the road while he was driving it, and finally Mr. Muhammad had to entreat Malcolm to take some NOI money and buy a new one. Still Malcolm resisted. In the end Brother Captain Joseph went out and bought it for him. Malcolm loved it; it was the dark blue Oldsmobile. The pride he took in that car, though, didn't alter the fact of his humility. "I didn't want to get the car," Malcolm later told me and the other assistant ministers, "because I didn't want the other ministers in the Nation to be jealous that Mr. Muhammad didn't also buy a car for any of them." Like the publicity, like the media attention, like the image, the new car was a Joseph's coat.

The public doesn't remember the humility of Brother Minister Malcolm. The public remembers the spellbinding Malcolm X, the fiery orator. It remembers the speeches and catchphrases like "by any means necessary." The Malcolm I remember most is not found in his speeches. The man I knew lived off the stage, away from the microphone. Malcolm seemed to me to be most comfortably himself, and most at home, in the temple. In my mind's eye I see him again standing at the blackboard with the chalk between his thumb and forefinger. I hear him teaching, I recall him ministering. The lessons Malcolm taught were simple ones, ultimately, and he lived his life by them: Be honest. Harm no one, and take nothing that is not yours. Treat others as you would be treated by them. Practice charity. Exercise self-control. Avoid extremes, keep a middle path. Pay your taxes. Obey the law.

To my knowledge there was only one exception to prove Malcolm's rules. He tended to ignore speed limits on open highways. This infringement of the law also sometimes involved a ruse. Whenever Malcolm was driving any distance, he would hang a cross from his rearview mirror and place his Bible on the dashboard; he might keep a clerical collar handy, too. Then, if he was stopped by the police for speeding, he would tell the officer he was sorry but he was late and rushing to a meeting where he had some good Christian colored people coming out to pray. He might quote some Bible verses as well. Malcolm pointed out to us that the officer, who would most likely be white, would never ticket a black preacher speeding down the highway in order to secure the necks of some so-called negroes in the noose of the white man's Christianity. Besides that, added Malcolm, preachers don't get speeding tickets. If by any chance Malcolm ever had been stopped, the officer would surely have thought he had just ticketed a good and upright man, a sincere and honest minister. He would not have thought wrong.

Los Angeles,
April 1962

On April 28, 1962, the Saturday edition of the *Los Angeles Times* described a shooting incident at the city's NOI mosque the night before as a "blazing gunfight" between policemen and black Muslims. The *Times* did not mention that only the police were armed, one reason why, perhaps, the vastly outnumbered police squad suffered only one casualty while the Muslims reported one brother dead and six others with serious or critical gunshot wounds. The newspaper's misleading and inaccurate coverage of the incident prompted Malcolm X to charge that the *Times*, a member of the white press, had colluded with LAPD Chief William J. Parker in suppressing the facts of the case and distorting its truth.

What had begun as police harassment ended in police gunfire. At 11:15 P.M., after the Friday night meeting at the Los Angeles mosque, two Muslim brothers were accosted by two white policemen who evidently suspected the Muslims of burglary or theft. The two Muslims at that moment happened to be unloading suits from the back of an automobile parked about a block away from the mosque; one of them owned a drycleaning establishment. Flustered in his attempt to explain himself, one of the brothers was talking with his hands. Objecting to the Muslim's nervous gestures, one of the policemen started mauling him. There was a scuffle. A shot was fired, and an alarm went out. A police squad answered. Instead of converging at the scene of the incident, however, the police gathered farther down the block, at the mosque itself.

They approached the site with their guns drawn and firing. Ronald Stokes, the secretary of the mosque, rushed out onto the sidewalk. He was asking the police what they wanted when they shot him through the heart. He fell to the sidewalk, and the police proceeded to beat him repeatedly on the head with their nightsticks. Then they handcuffed him. Stokes's body was left lying on the sidewalk for forty-five more minutes. The police meanwhile stormed into the mosque. Six more Muslim brothers, not one of them armed or even trying to defend himself, were shot in the foray. One was left completely paralyzed.

Malcolm himself had founded and helped to organize the Los Angeles mosque five years earlier. (The Los Angeles mosque was founded as Temple Number Twenty-seven. In December 1961, after returning from a tour of Muslim countries in the Middle East and Africa, Elijah Muhammad issued a directive that all NOI temples should thereafter be called mosques. Thus, too, New York Temple Number Seven became Mosque Number Seven.) Malcolm's personal affiliation with the Los Angeles mosque sharpened his embitterment. He may indeed have wanted to call for retaliatory measures or announce to the Los Angeles black Muslim community that the time for holy warfare, the long awaited days of Armageddon, had arrived. Elijah Muhammad, however, had not dispatched Malcolm to Los Angeles to stir Muslim blood or incite riots. Malcolm flew to the troubled city under instructions from Elijah Muhammad not to provoke but to prevent further violence. Upon his arrival on Saturday, April 28, Malcolm openly criticized the city's press and police force, but he did not speak of retaliation. Throughout his stay, as instructed, he took the NOI position that Allah, not the black Muslim community, would mete out just punishment upon the guilty. Not unfrustrated by the NOI's apolitical stance, Malcolm returned to New York a week later, after delivering the address at the funeral services for Ronald Stokes.

* * *

"Cool it," Malcolm said, "Mr. Muhammad told me to cool it." Malcolm was taken aback by that. He had gone out to Los Angeles the day after Stokes was killed, *Benjamin Karim recalls*, with his heart full of grief and his mind fixed on justice.

Malcolm mourned deeply for Ronald Stokes. He mourned the murder in cold blood of an unarmed, defenseless brother that the Los Angeles police would call a justifiable homicide committed in the line of duty. Police duty had likewise wounded six other innocent Muslim brothers. Duty had totally paralyzed one of them. As Malcolm saw it, Stokes and the others had been shot not because they were black Muslims but because they were black, period. A few weeks later, at a protest rally against police brutality, Malcolm would point out that the police don't ask your religion before they club you on the side of your head. That you're black is reason enough.

Malcolm had no sooner gotten from the Los Angeles airport into the city than he was making public statements about the white press covering up police brutality. He was angry, he was torn up by Stokes's death, and it showed. His bitter remarks were widely publicized. They were making Mayor Yorty's city and its police force sound about as progressive as redneck Mississippi in the fifties. They were riling people up on both sides of the color line. Resentment and anger, for years lying dormant in the city's black community, were beginning to flare up openly. Fearful that Malcolm's inflammatory rhetoric would trigger new violence in the city's ghetto, the police department was constantly in contact with the mayor's office. The police chief or, more probably, Mayor Yorty himself telephoned Mr. Muhammad and asked him to call Malcolm off. So Mr. Muhammad telephoned Malcolm. He told Malcolm to tone down his rhetoric.

He told him he didn't want the NOI involved in any more bloodshed or violence. He told him not to interfere in the racial politics of Los Angeles. He called Malcolm back to New York.

Malcolm came back after Stokes's funeral. He brought back with him a photograph that had been taken of Stokes's head after the autopsy. Malcolm had the photograph blown up as big as a wall. At rallies he would set it up on an easel and point out to his audience the holes and grooves from the policemen's nightsticks in Ronald Stokes's skull, which had been stitched back together again after the postmortem. Those scars and fissures would demonstrate to the rally the hypocrisy of the law and the inhumanity of the officers who were supposed to be protecting us. It may have upset Mr. Muhammad that Malcolm was using the photograph to such effect, but Malcolm felt strongly that something had to be done, at the very least that a protest had to be voiced against the murderous brutality imaged in that stark black-and-white blowup of Ronald Stokes's stitched-up head.

What Malcolm really wanted to do was fight fire with fire. He would have liked to have been able to retaliate against the police violence in a politically consequential way. Malcolm made it clear to us that retaliating against violence is not initiating it. (Malcolm would never have initiated a violent act, nor did he ever actually commit one for any reason in the years that I knew him.) Under extreme circumstances, Malcolm believed, extreme measures are justified. Sometimes, in order to survive, we have no alternative other than to retaliate. He illustrated such situations with a simple metaphor. If a dog runs up on you and it's barking and growling, Malcolm said, you back up or you back off. If the dog continues threatening you, baring its teeth and snarling, you back up some more. If, however, the dog persists until you can't back up another step and you have no choice but to turn and face its hate, then the time has come to retaliate. Cornered, denied any further retreat by your enemy, you call on your courage and you defend yourself, you strike back, and if you see murder in that dog's eye, you kill. Malcolm felt that the police in Los Angeles and New York, in Cleveland and Atlanta, in Phoenix and Boston, were continually pushing black people, not just Muslims, into corners with indiscriminate harassment, brutality, and murder. They would continue to do so, too, he believed, until we struck back and took a stand for justice.

Any number of Muslim brothers from any mosque anywhere in America would have been prepared at a moment's notice and at the cost of his own life, if necessary, to fly out to California in the cause of Islamic justice. Muslims don't believe in turning the other cheek. They believe in an eye for an eye, a life for a life. Blood vengeance is a matter of honor in the Muslim code, and the honor eclipses any fear of death. Also, the agent of vengeance is held guiltless by Muslim law. Muslims could have justified an attack on a squad of police officers or the assassination of a Los Angeles policeman as an act of retribution as easily as the police justified gunshot wounds and murder as acts committed in the line of duty.

Malcolm, however, was not seeking Muslim eye-for-eye vengeance for Ronald Stokes any more than Mr. Muhammad would have allowed it. Malcolm saw the Stokes incident as part of a larger cause, and he wanted to bring it into the larger battle of the black people in America for social justice and their human rights. When he got to Los Angeles, certainly, Malcolm did want to stir things up, because he wanted to wake up blacks to their condition in America. Mr. Muhammad, however, called Malcolm off. Mr. Muhammad did not want the NOI to be held responsible for any eruptions of violence among Los Angeles blacks. If a riot had broken out or had white blood been shed, the police in their turn would have retaliated by beating the black community back into submission to white authority. Perhaps then, though, America's blacks would have begun to see more clearly the true nature of their white oppressor. They might have responded to animosity with animosity. They might even have started the march to Armageddon. It didn't happen, though, and Mr. Muhammad didn't want it to happen. He told Malcolm to cool it.

The response of Mr. Muhammad and the NOI to the Ronald Stokes incident, I believe, brought into focus Malcolm's dissatisfaction with the apolitical stance of the Chicago leadership on social issues that significantly affected America's black population. Although Malcolm at no time during his ministry ever voiced that dissatisfaction publicly, he did sometimes allude to it in private. One night, as Brother Louis 2X and I were walking Malcolm from the mosque restaurant to his car, Malcolm stopped suddenly in the middle of the sidewalk and said to us, "You know, we talk about people being bitten by dogs and mowed down by fire hoses, we talk about our people being brutalized in the civil rights movement, and we haven't done anything to help them. We haven't done anything." The three of us had walked a few steps farther when Malcolm stopped again. "And now we've had one of our own brothers killed," he said, "and still we haven't done anything." Malcolm didn't blame Mr. Muhammad, but he didn't hide his dissatisfaction either. "We spout our militant revolutionary rhetoric and we preach Armageddon," he continued as we walked on, "but when our own brothers are brutalized or killed, we do nothing." We had reached Malcolm's car. "We just sit on our hands," he added as he opened the door. He slid into his Oldsmobile and headed for Queens. He wasn't pleased.

The closest the NOI came to an open political stand in the public arena during Mr. Muhammad's leadership, to my knowledge, was in Atlanta, when we founded our temple there. The Ku Klux Klan had threatened to disrupt any public Muslim ceremonies on this occasion by attacking the participants. We went down there nevertheless, thousands of us. Along with the police, the FOI in its impressive paramilitary form secured a four-block area surrounding the temple.

Brothers and sisters poured through the city streets toward the temple. Its seating could not accommodate most of them. They stood outside, on steps, on sidewalks, in the street. Atlanta felt our presence, and a mile away from the temple the Klan did too. They staged a protest but launched no attack.

In Atlanta we were of course acting only on behalf of our own. Politically, socially, economically, the NOI isolated itself from the world beyond the mosque. Firstly and fundamentally a religion, the NOI divorced itself entirely from the American political process. NOI members did not even vote, and when we took the message of Islam to other black people, we discouraged them from voting, too. The NOI was its own nation—the Nation of Islam—and it envisioned for black Muslims a separate territory within the United States that would be subsidized for twenty-five years by the government of the United States in payment for the long outstanding debt on black slavery. Its objective being to separate itself as a nation independent from the United States, the NOI offered no support whatever to the civil-rights movement. The NOI did not want to integrate anything, it did not want to segregate anything. The NOI wanted to separate everything.

The NOI based its operations in economics. Economic independence for all Muslim brothers and sisters stood next to religious enlightenment among NOI priorities. The NOI strove to establish businesses in black communities that provided Muslims not only with goods and services but also with jobs. While the civil rights movement was trying to integrate lunch counters and restaurants, the NOI was running its own restaurants as well as a chain of Muslim bakeries. (The idea for the bakeries as a business venture originated with Malcolm; the first one was attached to the mosque restaurant on Long Island.) The NOI also farmed its own land and orchards, which supplied its own shops with produce. Whereas the civil rights movement wanted to integrate

schools, the NOI had established its own educational institu-
tions with black Muslim administrators and teachers. At the
center of the standardized NOI curriculum stood the study
of black civilization, *black* meaning nonwhite or non-Euro-
pean, as study included the cultures of Asia and Africa as
well as black America. Asia and Africa also figured significantly in NOI financial interests, as the Nation had developed a thriving import-export business and had holdings in
textile mills and other factories in the Far East as well as
Africa. The NOI was planning to build its own hospitals. It
operated its own bank. The civil rights movement, meanwhile, was trying to integrate public toilets.

The NOI and the civil rights movement had little common
ground on which to meet. Malcolm nonetheless sympathized
with the thousands of men and women in the movement, with
the black housewives and white student volunteers, with
those first few who rode buses and sat down at segregated
lunch counters, with the masses who marched and prayed
and sang and demonstrated. His speeches reflect the pain
and horror he felt for them as they faced the water hoses,
police dogs, and billy clubs. By the hundreds they were in-
jured. Some were maimed for life, some died for the cause.
Malcolm admired their courage, and he decried the brutality
they suffered at the hands of the law. He respected them, all
the thousands of marchers and workers, and especially the
college students. He did not respect their leaders, however.
He could not respect men who taught their thousands of followers not to fight back and defend themselves. Again and
again Malcolm asserted that if you were going to die or be
killed, you might as well die fighting and be killed protecting
yourself. We all believed that. Had the Ku Klux Klan attacked the NOI that day in Atlanta, you would not have seen
anyone taking it sitting down, literally, like a misguided
corps of passively resistant civil rights workers.

As Malcolm saw it, the civil rights leadership—men like
Roy Wilkins, James Farmer, A. Philip Randolph, and Mar-

tin Luther King, Jr.—may have had dreams, but they didn't have vision. They weren't revolutionaries, they were integrationists. They were talking swimming pools, not black economics. They could not imagine a separate and independent black state, because they were tools. Malcolm scorned the alliance of the established black leadership to the larger, more powerful white liberal establishment. Financed by the white liberal establishment, black civil rights leaders, Malcolm argued, were also controlled by that establishment. They were bought men. They didn't fight, they kowtowed.

King's policy of passive resistance, in Malcolm's view, could as easily have been dreamed up by our long-time white oppressor, although King credited Gandhi as his model. As Malcolm pointed out to us in one of his lectures at the mosque, Gandhi challenged British rule in India with five or six hundred million people behind him. Nonviolent but resistant, a native Indian elephant was sitting on a colonial English fly. In America, however, Malcolm said, the elephant is white, and it's sitting on us. Malcolm then wanted to know how you can be passive with a white elephant sitting on top of you. He wondered how you can be passive when you're being crushed under the weight of established white authority. He asked us how you can be passive in the face of a white militia and a white police force. He asked us how you can be passive.

Whenever Malcolm spoke about the police dogs being unleashed upon a crowd of civil rights demonstrators, some of them singing and some of them praying, all of them defenseless, he stirred us up. That day his words inspired some of the brothers to offer their services as instructors in the martial arts to the rank and file in the movement. They were ready then and there to head south so that they could teach the marchers to defend themselves. Except that the NOI did not in any way support the civil rights movement.

Whatever personal dissatisfaction with NOI policy that Malcolm may have been feeling he kept to himself, but he was beginning to speak more and more for himself, especially after the Ronald Stokes incident. From New York to Los Angeles hundreds of thousands of registered Muslims listened to what he spoke. He was, after all, second in command only to the Honorable Elijah Muhammad. So some listened jealously.

New York,
December 1963

Malcolm X substituted for the Messenger. The Honorable Elijah Muhammad had been scheduled to deliver the main address to an NOI rally at the Manhattan Center in New York on December 1, 1963. Out of respect for the memory of President John F. Kennedy, whose recent assassination on November 22 was mourned across America by blacks as well as whites, the national leader of the NOI had canceled his appearance but not the rally itself. He had also issued a directive instructing all NOI ministers neither to discuss nor to comment upon the assassination of the president. While Malcolm's address to the rally—"God's Judgment on White America"—did criticize presidential policy and the Kennedy administration, it made no reference to the events in Dallas nine days earlier. After the address Malcolm took questions from the floor. When a woman in the audience asked him what he thought of the Kennedy assassination, Malcolm replied that Kennedy "never foresaw that the chickens would come home to roost so soon."

The statement was ambiguous, but however it might be interpreted, Malcolm had clearly failed to heed Elijah Muhammad's directive. On December 4, 1963, Malcolm was suspended from the NOI for ninety days. Not only was Malcolm stripped of his ministry and thus forbidden to teach even outside the mosque, he was also officially silenced. No college lectures or speaking engagements, no statements to the press or media interviews, no public communications of any kind, were allowed. For ninety days Malcolm was denied the cogence of his voice. The ill-timed comment, it would appear, had provided the NOI leadership with the pretext it needed not merely to suspend a recalcitrant minister but in effect to disempower the increasingly visible and outspoken Malcolm X. And not for just ninety days.

On March 8, 1964, after the suspension had apparently been extended indefinitely, Malcolm X broke his silence. MALCOLM X SPLITS WITH MUHAMMAD announced page one of the *New York Times*. The *Times* went on to report Malcolm's plans to establish a black nationalist party that would cooperate with other local civil rights actions in order to heighten the political consciousness of African Americans and that would promote a policy of active self-defense, as opposed to nonviolence, in the face of white supremacy. To that end, on March 12, Malcolm X founded the Muslim Mosque, Incorporated.

* * *

For months you could see it coming, *says Benjamin Karim*. It was inevitable, Malcolm's split with Elijah Muhammad. You could hear it in his speeches, not so much in what was said as in what Malcolm was leaving out. When I first joined the temple in 1957, every idea, observation, parable, or fact was introduced into Malcolm's lectures by "Mr. Muhammad teaches us that . . ." Or Malcolm would conclude a thought with "Mr. Muhammad taught me that." Mr. Muhammad this and Mr. Muhammad that, you couldn't count the *Mr. Muhammads* or the times he'd say that "Mr. Muhammad taught me everything I know"—and more than anyone, Mr. Muhammad knew that wasn't true. It was Malcolm's way of paying his respect to his teacher. Five years later, though, you weren't hearing what Mr. Muhammad said or taught so much as before. How consciously Malcolm was more and more omitting Mr. Muhammad from his lectures I don't know, but I think it shows that Malcolm was beginning to feel the limitations of Mr. Muhammad's teachings and the restraints of the NOI. Malcolm's intellect had begun to outgrow NOI doctrine. Just as a baby moves into a larger world when it outgrows its mother's womb, Malcolm outgrew the NOI, and he had to move where his mind took him.

Malcolm was also being pushed. Forces outside himself and inside the NOI were conspiring first to suspend him from his ministry and then to oust him from the Nation entirely. In 1962 and 1963 the NOI leadership in Chicago was becoming increasingly nervous about Malcolm X. Malcolm's prominence in the media and his growing public popularity, which were winning the NOI impressive numbers of converts, alarmed rather than pleased the Chicago officials. They resented the media's treatment of Malcolm as the NOI's national spokesman second in power only to the Honorable Elijah Muhammad himself. They resented that new members for the most part were responding to Malcolm's leadership without reference to the Chicago chain of command. They resented that as the membership grew so did Malcolm's favor with Mr. Muhammad. The Chicago officials read any of Malcolm's NOI gains as their loss.

The Chicago leadership did have some cause for concern. Malcolm's special relationship with Mr. Muhammad as well as his friendship with the leader's second son and nominal successor, W.D. (Wallace) Muhammad, promised to place Malcolm in the top position of national power, or very close to it, upon Mr. Muhammad's death. That Mr. Muhammad suffered from chronic bronchitis, a condition that on several occasions in the early sixties brought him close to dying, added urgency to the concern of the Chicago officials. They had interests to protect. To support their extravagant lifestyles and to conceal their corruption they had to maintain control of the NOI. They knew Malcolm's high moral standards. They knew that they could not hope to bribe him into collusion. They knew that in the event of Mr. Muhammad's death all they could expect from Malcolm X was a thorough housecleaning in Chicago. Demanding a standard of morality no lower than his own, Malcolm would call them all to account and he would find them all lacking. The NOI would find itself with a new leadership. Perhaps they had heard what Malcolm often said: "You don't take tea for a fever." Certainly they feared Malcolm's strong moral medicine. With Malcolm in the NOI picture their future looked bleak.

At the Chicago headquarters, next in power to Mr. Muhammad stood John Ali, the national secretary of the NOI, and Supreme Captain Raymond Sharrieff. John Ali, who had been the secretary of Number Seven and had gone to the national office on Malcolm's recommendation, oversaw all the financial interests of the NOI. With a staff of accountants, bookkeepers, assistants, secretaries, typists, and clerks, he received and disbursed all the moneys that came into Chicago from NOI businesses and investments as well as dues, fees, and donations from the memberships in all the other mosques across America. He ran the Nation of Islam bank. Official NOI letters and communications between Chicago and the local mosques went through Ali's office. Ali's was a highly sensitive and influential position. When he visited other mosques, the FOI captains bowed down to him. They took their orders, however, from Supreme Captain Raymond Sharrieff.

Supreme Captain Raymond Sharrieff worked closely in the Chicago office with Mr. Muhammad's son, Elijah, Jr., and was married to Mr. Muhammad's daughter Ethel. Sharrieff commanded the paramilitary personnel of all the mosques. In national headquarters, as in the local mosques, ranked beneath the captain were lieutenants, second lieutenants, investigators, and privates, the rank and file of the FOI. All military directives and FOI policy decisions, all the rules and regulations enforced by captains of the local mosques, originated in the Chicago office of the supreme captain. The MGT was similarly organized and was headed by Supreme Captain Ethel Muhammad. Through the chain of command and communications in the FOI and MGT, then, from Chicago to New York to San Francisco, Albany, Pittsburgh, and Richmond, the NOI leadership was able to reach every brother and sister in the Nation. The NOI was as well structured and well supervised an organization as any arm of the federal government. Even though we carried no weapons, the FBI still classified us as a primary threat to the internal security of the United States.

The NOI had numerous sources of income. First of all, it had us, the entire NOI membership. Hundreds of thousands of brothers and sisters provided the NOI with its working capital. Every NOI member was obligated to donate at least twelve dollars a week to the Nation. In addition, each week every brother in the Nation was expected to sell his quota, fifty copies, of the NOI newspaper, *Muhammad Speaks*. Because many brothers were consistently failing to meet their weekly quotas, the leadership instituted a more expedient policy. Each week every brother himself was required to purchase the fifty copies of *Muhammad Speaks*, so that ultimately it didn't matter to the officials whether he managed to sell the papers or not. A brother was allowed to make a profit on his sales, however. Say that he bought the papers from the NOI at twenty cents each. He could then sell them at a quarter apiece and thus make a nickel on each—$2.50, if he sold them all. He usually didn't. With every brother in the temple out there on the streets trying to sell fifty newspapers each week, the competition became fierce and the weekly payments a burden. Each week you'd see more papers stacking up in your closet. It was discouraging. A lot of the brothers began to resent the NOI's newspaper policy. They were beginning to feel that an anonymous, money-hungry leadership in Chicago was trying to take advantage of their spiritual commitment to Islam and was giving them only reams of newsprint in return. Except for Mr. Muhammad, of course.

We all venerated the Messenger, and believed him infallible, for he had been taught by God in the person of Fard.

Fard, too, brought in revenue. Fard's birthday, which had been declared Saviour's Day by Mr. Muhammad back in 1934, was celebrated on February 26 with a national convention in Chicago. We would charter caravans of buses to make the trip with Minister Malcolm from New York to the national headquarters. (You could no longer put all the Muslims in New York in two cars and still have room for two more, as they used to say of Number Seven before Brother Malcolm's ministry.) At the convention we'd gather with all the other busloads of sisters and brothers from all over the United States and together we would commemorate the birth of our Saviour, the Prophet Fard, in the presence of his Messenger, the Honorable Elijah Muhammad. To mark the holiday, all registered Muslims, whether they attended the annual ceremonies or not, were required to make a donation of one hundred dollars or more to the NOI. Throughout the year the NOI also sponsored bazaars, fairs, FOI displays, and other special events to raise additional funds. "Money!" John Ali would say on every occasion he visited the New York mosque. "We need to raise more money."

The money went into NOI investments. In Chicago the NOI owned and managed apartment buildings, supermarkets, restaurants, a bank, a meat-packing plant. It manufactured clothes and developed real estate in Arizona. It ran an import-export business. It was laying the economic foundation of the Muslim nation. Mr. Muhammad wanted the NOI to show black people what they could do. Independently, in their own communities, by pooling their human resources and funds, they, too, could buy, build, own, manage, develop, run, and finance their own businesses. Mr. Muhammad used to say that black people should stop begging white people to take care of them, that they should get off welfare and get into the Nation. In the Nation, he said, they would discover that their freedom began in economic independence and dignity lay in their economic power. Mr. Muhammad encouraged black people to adopt the ways of Islam, to work and study and learn to better their economic condition, to build a Nation with an economic future that their children and grandchildren and great grandchildren would secure. It was a beautiful idea. It might have worked if the national leadership had not corrupted it with waste, greed, misman-agement, and self-interest.

Mr. Muhammad was ill, and the Chicago officials were getting drunk on wealth and power. They were mishandling their personal assets. They were misappropriating NOI funds. I had never before seen Malcolm truly angry until the day he placed a long-distance telephone call to John Ali in Chicago regarding the money—between thirty and forty thousand dollars—we had raised at Number Seven toward building a new mosque. Malcolm was fuming with anger. Ali had told him the money had been invested in some other venture. When Malcolm had asked him what other venture, Ali had replied offhandedly, "Oh, something or other." Mal-colm had pressed him further, and Ali had snapped back, "In what? In what! I don't have to tell you in what." Mal-colm said later that they probably needed some loose change to dress Ethel up in diamonds and mink for a fancy night on the town. He also said that the officials in Chicago were tak-ing advantage of Mr. Muhammad's illness to usurp control of the Nation. The NOI was becoming a criminal organization, he said.

Other than his ailing mentor, the only person in the Chi-cago mosque that Malcolm respected was W.D. Muhammad, Mr. Muhammad's son Wallace. Minister Wallace stood in sharp moral contrast to his brothers Herbert and Elijah, Jr., and to the NOI leadership as a whole. He was essentially an honest man, a humble man, whose integrity had always set him outside the circle of power in Chicago. Had Wallace been willing to compromise a little with his principles, he could have walked into the Salaam, Chicago's famous Muslim restaurant, whenever he pleased and taken out of the cash drawer whatever he pleased. He could have walked into the Nation's bank and in minutes have financed a mansion his brothers might have coveted. Instead he lived in a modest house, and to keep the door to his refrigerator closed, he had to tie a length of rope around it.

Minister Wallace had been taught Arabic as a child and he had read the Koran in its original language. He had grown up knowing, then, that the Koran did not substantiate much of the doctrine his father was teaching under the name of Islam. Wallace preached what he believed, and he believed what he read in the Koran. As the Koran taught nothing of Fard, let alone of his divinity, Wallace did not teach that Fard was God or that Fard had ever spoken to God in the guise of the Prophet. As the Koran failed to support Elijah Muhammad's claim of direct lineage to the Prophet Muhammad, the founder of Islam in the seventh century, Wallace could not accept that his father was by birthright the Messenger of Allah. If Wallace also spoke his heterodoxy, he would be suspended for thirty days. A month later he'd come back. He'd preach, he'd get reported, he'd be out again for thirty days. It was comical, but Minister Wallace was no fool.

When Mr. Muhammad fell ill in 1962, Minister Wallace started pulling Malcolm's coat about Islamic doctrine and the NOI. He lectured Malcolm on the Koran; he began teaching him Arabic. Malcolm listened, and his addresses in the mosque about that time began to show it. Not only was Malcolm referring less frequently to Mr. Muhammad, he wasn't mentioning Fard at all. ("Who do you think I am?" asked Fard in a dark, deep voice, according to one story Malcolm used to tell. Elijah Poole had come from rural Georgia with only a third-grade education, but he knew, and he replied to Fard, "You are God." In that moment was Poole converted, and appointed. He became God's messenger.) I was not the only one who noticed that Malcolm no longer spoke of Fard or who knew that Wallace had Malcolm's ear. So did the

Chicago leadership, which put to immediate use any ammunition at hand in order to forward its whispering campaign with Mr. Muhammad against Malcolm X.

Wallace, meanwhile, was sharing with Malcolm his firsthand observations of the maneuverings inside the Chicago mosque. Wallace corroborated Malcolm's view that the national leadership was taking advantage of his father's bronchitis to gain continually more authority over NOI operations. To the same end, Wallace also told Malcolm, the top-ranking officials were exploiting their knowledge of Mr. Muhammad's infidelities. Wallace then revealed to Malcolm, or confirmed any rumors Malcolm may have heard, that Mr. Muhammad had fathered six illegitimate children with as many young office secretaries. Unsettled, disappointed, confused, Malcolm learned, too, that he knew all six women and in some cases had recommended them to Mr. Muhammad. He felt responsible, he felt sick. I remember the day Malcolm received this troubling piece of news from Wallace. I came upon Malcolm in the mosque restaurant. He was sitting with his elbows on the counter and his head bowed. He was pressing his forehead hard against the palms of his quivering hands. "I've just come from the doctor," said Malcolm, his voice trembling slightly and his head pounding with migraine, "I heard something today that affected me so badly I thought my brain cells were bleeding." What he had heard he refused to tell me. In fact, I knew nothing about Mr. Muhammad's infidelities until January 1964, just six months or so before Malcolm went public with the information. I knew no less than the other assistant ministers or the general membership. Captain Joseph knew, though. So did Louis Farrakhan, and a number of other NOI ministers. Most of them knew even before Malcolm. Everyone who knew the secret had to keep it a secret even from himself.

Once he had digested the news, Malcolm did come up with a strategy. He called together the assistant ministers at Number Seven for some special instruction. He told us no secrets, but he did ask us to introduce into our lectures stories that showed holy men in not an altogether favorable light. He suggested we might for instance discuss Noah, who retained his goodness in the eyes of God even though he lay down naked in wanton drunkenness, or we might tell the story of Lot in the incestuous bed of his daughters. Malcolm wanted us to plant the seeds of ideas in the minds of the brothers and sisters about the reality of imperfection even in prophets and holy men. That way their minds would be better prepared to deal with any shocking revelations from the press about the Muslim leadership. Had the press printed the story of Mr. Muhammad's infidelities and illegitimate children, the news would have shaken the faith of every mosque in the Nation. Adultery violated Muslim law, and the NOI exempted no one from the laws of the Nation, supposedly. Suspension for a single instance of adultery could run from one to five years. Conceivably Mr. Muhammad could have been suspended for life, yet we had been taught to believe in the One True Messenger's infallibility.

The Messenger's fallibility provided the leadership in Chicago with the leverage it needed to wrest further control over the NOI from Mr. Muhammad's grip. The national officials had Mr. Muhammad morally paralyzed. He could challenge their misdeeds only at the risk of his reputation. Mr. Muhammad's situation reminded me of the old Chinese piano-wire trick. Piano wire is tied first around the victim's chest, then drawn up taut and looped around his neck. If the victim breathes, the wire tightens around his neck. The victim decapitates himself. If, on the other hand, he holds his breath, he suffocates. The national leadership would have liked to have had Malcolm in a similar position.

Malcolm's comment regarding the Kennedy assassination was no piano wire, but it did the trick. It gave the national officials the advantage they needed to prize Brother Minister Malcolm out of the NOI.

Malcolm had never been quiet about Kennedy. Even the day he made the comment, a Sunday, December 1, 1963, Malcolm spoke about Kennedy in his address to the rally. For months he had been accusing President Kennedy of willful deception in his stand on civil rights issues. Kennedy's policy on integration had little to do with the political or social realities of African Americans, as Malcolm saw it, and nothing to do with economic opportunity. It had to do with using public toilets, said Malcolm, and all the blacks he knew, he said, could build their own toilets. With as little as a toilet and a lunch counter Kennedy had nevertheless hoodwinked the black leaders in the civil rights movement. With empty words and vague promises and white money he had manipulated men like CORE's James Farmer, Whitney Young of the Urban League, Roy Wilkins at the NAACP, and SCLC leader Martin Luther King, Jr., and reduced them to ineffectual Uncle Toms, Malcolm asserted. Malcolm often compared the black Muslim movement to a wildfire raging out of control in a parched national forest. He likened the established black civil rights leadership, on the other hand, to a backfire built by Kennedy to check the flame of Islam sweeping through the land. The March on Washington, said Malcolm, was just another backfire fueled by Kennedy to prevent the spread of the Islamic blaze. Malcolm's fire, certainly, blazed on. While Kennedy was trying to enact civil rights legislation in the capital and at the same time to placate the white community in the South, Malcolm was telling the world about the police dogs and police brutality being unleashed on defenseless citizens in America's sunlit streets. People in every segment of American society were beginning to listen to Malcolm, too. He was speaking plainly and he was making sense. He was creating problems for Kennedy. In 1963 Kennedy told a special news conference with seven journalists that if the United States didn't hurry up and get the segregation bars down, all the blacks in America would be following Malcolm X. That comment made the front page of the *New York Times*. So did Kennedy's remark about Malcolm and an experimental bomber, the BX, that had been causing the government some problems. First we had problems with the BX, Kennedy observed, and now we have problems with Malcolm X.

Critical though Malcolm was of the president, Kennedy remained very popular with black people. They grieved his passing deeply, and Mr. Muhammad felt that comment upon the assassination of the president by an NOI minister might stir up the animosity of blacks against the Muslims. So he issued a directive forbidding it. Malcolm never planned to challenge Mr. Muhammad's directive. He made no mention of the assassination in the "God's Judgment on White America" speech he presented that Sunday at the Manhattan Center. After the speech, when that woman in the audience asked him about Kennedy's assassination, he just automatically answered her. He said straight out that it was a matter of the chickens coming home to roost. What he meant, I think, was that violence was only breeding more violence in American society and it had culminated in the death of an American president at the hands of a private citizen. What he meant didn't matter to the national secretary, John Ali. He was attending the rally that day, and he reported back to Chicago immediately. Three days later, on December 4, Malcolm was suspended by Mr. Muhammad for ninety days. I was in the temple when the call from Chicago came through. We were told that if Malcolm came back to the temple after the suspension, we should give him a job washing dishes in the restaurant.

Throughout the ninety silent days of his suspension Malcolm remained loyal to Mr. Muhammad. He did not attack or expose the Dear Holy Apostle, as Mr. Muhammad was also known, and he continued, as he always would, to respect him as his teacher. In Chicago, meanwhile, the NOI officials were calling Malcolm X a hypocrite. Louis Farrakhan in Boston was calling him a hypocrite. Minister James Shabazz in Newark was calling him a hypocrite. In every issue of *Muham-mad Speaks* someone was calling Malcolm a hypocrite. Since his suspension the hypocrite Malcolm had been speaking rumors and spreading lies about the Messenger, said the NOI newspaper, without disclosing what Malcolm was supposedly saying. The newspaper also ran a cartoon showing Malcolm's head bouncing up and down like a basketball and blabbing, blabbing, blabbing, blabbing. Like the articles, it didn't indicate what Malcolm might be blabbing. For one thing, it would have been unwise to repeat rumors that some Muslims, especially in Chicago, might not find entirely unfounded. For another, it was unnecessary. To prove Malcolm's hypocrisy, the NOI newspaper only had to establish that Malcolm was blabbing, not what he was blabbing, because there was nothing that could possibly be said against the Honorable—and morally infallible—Elijah Muhammad. In another issue of *Muhammad Speaks*, Louis Farrakhan, the man whom Malcolm loved like a brother, called for the death of the hypocrite Malcolm X. If you knew what Malcolm X was saying about the One True Messenger of Allah, said the article that did not need to mention either adultery or secretaries or illegitimate children, you would kill the hypocrite. And a year later a band of Muslim zealots did. The Koran teaches Muslims to kill hypocrites wherever they may find them.

Malcolm's comment indirectly, and sadly, eventually cost him another close friend. Cassius Clay had been introduced to Islam by his brother Rudolph, and he had joined Number Seven because he admired the teaching of Brother Minister Malcolm. A friendship developed, and at first it seemed unaffected by Malcolm's suspension. In January 1964, when he was preparing for the world heavyweight boxing championship match with Sonny Liston, Clay insisted that Malcolm visit him for a week at his training camp in Florida. Clay wanted his spiritual adviser with him the next month as well, at the title fight itself. To win, Clay said, he needed Brother

Minister Malcolm's support and prayers. Malcolm went. (No
one in the NOI leadership bothered to attend the title match
in Miami that February; they had not expected Clay to upset
Liston for the title.) Not long after Clay's victory, back in
New York, Malcolm and I were driving down St. Nicholas
Avenue with the Sunday night broadcast of *Muhammad
Speaks* on the car radio. We had just crossed 125th Street
when Mr. Muhammad announced that from this day forward
Cassius Clay would be known as Muhammad Ali. Malcolm
laughed at that. He laughed, and he said, "That's political."
Very few Muslims were given Arabic holy names by the Mes-
senger. We were given X's. At the time of our Saviour's com-
ing we would receive from Fard our true holy names. With
the name Muhammad Ali, then, the Messenger was bestowing
upon Clay one of black Islam's highest honors. At the same
time Mr. Muhammad was ensuring Clay's allegiance to the
Nation that had in essence already betrayed Malcolm X.
Malcolm laughed, but he knew he had lost an ally and friend.
It was political.

At Number Seven, during the suspension, administration
of the mosque was taken over by Captain Joseph. Under
direct orders from John Ali and Raymond Sharrieff in Chicago, Captain Joseph was constantly urging the mosque's
staff of assistant ministers to speak out against Malcolm and
his hypocrisy. I had never known anyone to speak out
against a brother after he had been suspended; it violated
our code of honor. I couldn't believe, either, that we were
being asked to condemn Malcolm on charges that had not
been heard before an NOI court or, barring that, for rumors
that were continually being alleged but never being specified.
It was not Islamic, I said to Captain Joseph, to speak out
against any brother in such circumstances. Were I to slander
a brother without proof at any other time, by Muslim law I
would be at once suspended. I told Captain Joseph that we
had also been taught by Islam to want for our brothers only
what we wanted for ourselves. You would not eat the flesh off

the back of your dead brother, I told him, yet in a sense I was being asked to do just that, to feed on the flesh of my brother, to prey on the good name of Malcolm X. Captain Joseph did not alter his instructions. He obeyed all orders from Chicago.

My personal conscience got caught in the chain of command. Certainly I did not want to speak out against Malcolm, but I did not feel ready to abandon my ministry or the mosque. So, for a while, I did nothing. Nothing, however, resolved nothing. The only way to resolve the conflict warring inside myself, Malcolm counseled me, was to determine for myself on which side truth and justice lay, and in the light of that knowledge to make my choice and declare myself. One thing daily became more clear. If I was not going to toe the NOI line and speak out against Malcolm's hypocrisy, I was going to have to leave the mosque. Soon I would have no choice but one way or the other to declare myself.

I made my choice. In my mind I had made it even before I heard about Luqman, but I had not declared it. Sometime in February 1964 Brother Luqman, an explosives specialist, received orders from FOI Captain Joseph to wire a bomb to the ignition of Malcolm's car. This was no scare tactic. The device was meant to be detonated when Malcolm—no other driver or passengers were taken into account—started the car, and it was meant to kill. Luqman did not follow Captain Joseph's orders. Instead he reported the plot to Malcolm and quit the NOI. Someone reported it, too, to the *Amsterdam News*, which ran the whole story.

I read the story at first with disbelief. Then I read it with rage, pain, tears, disgust. I read it again the following Sunday as I sat behind Brother Henry at Mosque Number Seven and wondered sadly what had become of our Islamic brotherhood. At the podium Brother Henry was making announcements over a hand mike. A brother and a sister were getting married, so-and-so had been taken ill, the mosque was planning to sponsor a bazaar, and suddenly I was out of order. I was standing up there beside him, beside Brother Henry at the podium. "Excuse me, Brother Minister," I said, as I took away his microphone. "Excuse me, but can I say a word real quick?" Brother Minister Henry looked startled. He looked at me, at the mike, at the newspaper in my hand. He did not really want to oblige, but he didn't object. *"Assalaam alaikum,"* I acknowledged the audience. And then I said, "What I am going to say to you is the truth of what I feel." The mosque was full, with people standing along the walls, and everyone was listening attentively, in part because they realized I was talking out of order. "If you can believe what the *New York Times*, which is a white newspaper, has been saying against Brother Malcolm," I said, referring to a recent article NOI ministers had been eagerly quoting, "then I can believe what the *Amsterdam News*, a black newspaper written totally for blacks, says about Captain Joseph sending out Brother Luqman to plant a bomb in Brother Malcolm's car." I threw the rolled-up newspaper down onto the podium. I left the platform, and I walked out of the mosque. About a third of the audience, as disenchanted with the organization as I, applauded and walked out with me.

Throughout the suspension the NOI leadership continued to widen the rift between Malcolm and Mr. Muhammad. At the end of its ninety days the suspension became indefinite, the Chicago officials claiming that Malcolm had violated the silencing by speaking lies and rumors. A few days later Malcolm announced his split with the Nation of Islam. He left the Nation not out of any disaffection from Mr. Muhammad but because of his disillusionment with the national leadership. For the same reason about one-third of the membership nationwide sided with Malcolm and severed ties with the NOI; likewise one-third of the close to three thousand Muslims registered at Number Seven. One-third of the NOI membership was willing to risk the safe harbor it had found inside the Nation and to set out on uncharted waters with the man who had always dynamically led and inspired them.

Remembering
Malcolm

At a Sunday meeting of New York Mosque Number Seven in February 1964, Assistant Minister Benjamin declared himself. He chose the side on which for him truth and justice, loyalty, honor, pride, and genuine brotherhood lay. When he spoke that day for Malcolm, he spoke not only for the minister and teacher he knew and admired. He also spoke for a man who had become a friend, a man he could neither forget nor abandon after their seven years together inside the temple. Benjamin Karim remembers the man he knew then and the minister he assisted at Number Seven.

* * *

I remember when I was substituting as the minister at the Washington mosque and shuttling two or three times a week between the capital and New York. After the meeting and the customary socializing with the membership at the mosque, I'd have to rush to catch the last Eastern Airlines shuttle back to LaGuardia at midnight. On landing I'd go directly from the airport to Malcolm's home in East Elmhurst so that I could go over all that day's proceedings in the Washington mosque. It would be late by the time I'd get there, at least one thirty usually, but these sessions could never wait till the next day. Despite the hour, when he opened the door to his quiet house, Malcolm would still be alert, as wide awake as he was at noon. He'd be wearing a

165

dark maroon robe over his suit trousers and white shirt, and he'd have changed from his dress shoes into house slippers. I'd follow him up the stairs to his study in the attic, where Malcolm spent most of the time that he wasn't at the mosque.

Malcolm's attic room told you this was a place where someone worked and thought. I think you'd have felt Malcolm's presence in his study even when he wasn't there, and when he was, the walls, it seemed, could barely contain his intellectual energy. The bookshelves told you some of what Malcolm was reading or had read—and if you looked at the pages and bindings, you knew those books really had been read—from the complete Shakespeare, which he loved for the language, to histories of the Moors in Spain to astronomy to Mendel's genetics. On the shelves you could find, too, some of what Malcolm had said. Malcolm often stood in for Mr. Muhammad on the Sunday night *Muhammad Speaks* radio broadcasts. After recording his address for the half-hour program, Malcolm would send one copy of the tape out to Chicago for the broadcast and keep one for himself in New York. Malcolm also often taped his lectures at meetings and rallies so that he could review them afterward. Up in the solitude of his attic study he would play them back and analyze them, and then maybe revise them, perfect them. Malcolm worked constantly to perfect both what he spoke and how he spoke it. Speaking to people was Malcolm's life, his voice the power the NOI tried to silence when they extended the suspension indefinitely. After I'd leave, depending on the hour, Malcolm might play some classical music and work a little while longer at the index cards and reference books lying open on his desk or he might go directly to bed.

Just before dawn Malcolm would again be up so that he could say his first prayers at sunrise. Like Einstein and Edison, Malcolm did not need but four hours of sleep each night. Still, he never lacked energy for his work. Between his time studying at home and the long hours attending to his ministry at the mosque Malcolm regularly worked sixteen or eighteen hours a day, and sometimes twenty. I don't remember, though, that he ever took a vacation, other than his visit to Cassius Clay's training camp, or that he took a day off sick. I don't remember Malcolm ever being seriously ill. He did have days, however, that he'd be feeling terrible.

As heavy as Malcolm's schedule was, especially those years in the sixties before his suspension, it was bound on occasion to run him down, but it never knocked him out. Malcolm always met his commitments. I sometimes wondered how. I remember times before a speech or lecture when Malcolm would be so tired and hoarse that he could barely speak to me sitting next to him. When he'd get up to the podium, though, he would soon be preaching with such force you'd think he wouldn't need a microphone to reach even a deaf person in the last row of the audience. Of course, after he'd finish, what voice he had left sounded more like a croak than a whisper. In case his throat went hoarse Malcolm always carried a small bottle of Listerine with him. (He carried it for his breath as well; as Malcolm pointed out to us, fasting till your evening meal does nothing at all to sweeten a brother's breath.)

A night that I particularly remember during one of those periods that Malcolm was really being overtaxed by his schedule he and I were driving up to Bridgeport for a meeting at the mosque. Suddenly we veered. Malcolm quickly righted the car and then pulled over to the side of the road. We had been driving inside the speed limit, but Malcolm had been driving himself into exhaustion. With a heavy sigh he leaned back behind the wheel. "Can you drive, Brother Benjamin?" he asked me. I told him I could, that I'd learned to drive in 1950, when I joined the air force, and that I'd never had an accident. "Do you have a license, Brother Benjamin?" he asked. I answered no, and he replied, "Well, then, you can't drive, can you, Brother Benjamin?" Dead-tired as he was, he wouldn't let me drive without a license. He pulled himself out of the car and shook himself awake in the cold

Connecticut night. He gargled with some Listerine to freshen his mouth. He perked himself up further with a few deep breaths of the chilly air. Feeling a little better, he slid back in behind the wheel of his Oldsmobile and drove the remaining eighteen miles or so to Bridgeport, where he lectured with such vitality that you would have thought the man had just risen from a restful bed. At the blackboard or at the lectern Malcolm never flagged. Teaching exhilarated him. To lead his Muslim sisters and brothers out of centuries of ignorance, to enlighten their minds and enrich their lives with vision and pride, excited him. However tired or terrible he might feel, Malcolm would not fail to meet his commitment to them, his brothers and sisters both inside and out of the Nation.

Malcolm dressed for his people. So did all the assistant ministers and FOI staff. Our suits and ties, our uniforms, did more than identify our brotherhood. They also showed our respect for each other and our people. In general we all wore whatever color suit Captain Joseph stipulated, either brown or gray or navy blue. Malcolm had suits that he preferred for particular occasions. Whenever he wore his dark blue suit with a red tie, for instance, you knew you could expect him to deliver a memorable lecture. We used to call it the Minister's branding suit because that day Malcolm intended his words to leave an indelible impression on the minds of every brother and sister. Malcolm wore any suit the way you would a uniform. The trousers would be perfectly creased, the jacket pressed, the white shirt fresh, his tie knotted neatly and right up to the neck—always. You might catch Malcolm with his shirt tails hanging out over a pair of dungarees if he was pitching in to help a brother paint his house or you might discover him in overalls, and his face smudged with grease, when he pushed himself out from under a brother's car, but you would never find him—or any of us—with his tie loosened around his neck. ("What size shirt do you wear, brother?" he would ask you the one and only time you'd loosen your tie at the neck. "Fifteen and a half," you might reply. Then he'd ask you what size shirt you were wearing that day. Maybe a little mystified, you'd again reply fifteen and a half. "Well," Malcolm would return, "you'd better go out and buy yourself a sixteen, because it looks to me like you need more room around the neck.")

Malcolm's tie was properly knotted and nicely matched to the brown suit jacket and brown shoes that he was wearing one time that I especially remember because he was also wearing blue suit trousers. I don't think anyone in the temple had ever before seen, or would ever again see, Malcolm at the rostrum in a jacket and trousers from two entirely different suits. He must have been really preoccupied that day as he himself didn't even notice the mismatch until he read the note sent up to the rostrum by Captain Joseph. "You're out of uniform," read the note. "You've got on your brown suit jacket with blue pants." Malcolm looked surprised. Then he looked at his jacket and trousers. He laughed, and taught us a lesson about keeping our consciousness of the simple, everyday, familiar things around us, whatever other weighty matters might be demanding our concentration. At least he hadn't shown up like Einstein with a sock tied around his neck.

Time hounded Malcolm's consciousness. One day Malcolm noticed that his gold, spring-wound wristwatch had begun to lose time. He had evidently but uncharacteristically neglected to wind it. So that he could reset it correctly, he asked one of the brothers the time. After checking his watch and reading Malcolm the time, the brother added that he kept his watch running five minutes fast so that he would be wherever he had to be five minutes before he had to be there. That way he'd not be late. Malcolm responded with surprising vehemence. He told the young brother never to set his watch ahead of the correct time. Being on time, said Malcolm, did not mean arriving five minutes early. That was merely wasting time, he said. He explained that our lives are measured by time, so we shouldn't lose the time that we

might spend any number of times every day waiting five minutes for a time that according to our watches has already
been and gone. After that all the brothers set their watches
on the correct time.

Being on time did not mean arriving five minutes late,
either. Malcolm did not tolerate unpunctuality. On one of
the occasions that the mosque was sponsoring an excursion
to a special NOI meeting with Mr. Muhammad in Philadelphia we chartered several buses so that the brothers and
sisters from Number Seven could travel as a group with
Brother Malcolm and the assistant ministers. One person arrived for the buses at the mosque a half hour after our
scheduled departure time, and so made every other one of us
thirty minutes late. We were all put out. I could tell Malcolm
was rankled, but he hid his irritation until our next meeting
at the mosque. That Sunday he informed us that Number
Seven was not one of those so-called negro organizations that
accommodated itself to one person's behindhand habits or
another's lackadaisical pace. Punctuality, he said, demonstrated Muslim self-discipline and attested to our respect for
sisters and brothers who valued their time. Malcolm then
announced that on all future excursions chartered buses
would depart no more than five minutes after the scheduled
hour, no matter who had not arrived. A half dozen brothers
and sisters arrived six or seven minutes late for our next
excursion. They missed the bus.

Malcolm had no time for nothing. I don't think Malcolm's
mind ever stopped. His eyes seemed always to be quick with
concern or alive with thought, even when he was relaxing
over a cup of coffee and a piece of bean pie. He could be
easily matching someone's wit or fully enjoying a lengthy
anecdote at the same time that his mind was running on
another, totally different track, and his hands were rarely
quiet. All the while we'd be sitting at a table in the temple
restaurant or in Malcolm's booth at 22 West, Malcolm would
be doodling. On the face of his napkin, from the edge to the

fold, he'd be sketching his minute lines intricately into a geometrical design. He would take his napkins with him when we'd leave the coffee house or restaurant because, he said, he didn't want anyone trying to psychoanalyze him on the basis of aimless inky scribbling on a paper napkin. He gave me some of the doodles. You could study them and read into them just about anything you wanted, but you could only barely touch the subtlety of the mind that produced them.

If he wasn't doodling, Malcolm was doing everything else you've seen an earnest man do in a hospital waiting room while his first child is being born. He was pacing, he was tapping his fingers and feet. He was like a piece of jelly, and his fourth cup of pale coffee was turning as cold as the three before it. He was chattery. One minute he'd be talking about temple business and the next he would again be telling us— Captain Joseph, Brother Henry, and me—that he had decided to name the child after the king of the Huns, who was also known as the Scourge of God, if the child was a boy, although you couldn't really predict these things as the boy might in fact be a girl, but he somehow hadn't been counting on that, or so he guessed, because he hadn't come up with any other name than that. At one point I took Malcolm for a walk outside the hospital. I tried to distract him with the November night and to occupy his mind with plans for upcoming events at the temple. (It was 1958. The night was full of expectancy, and neither of us would have imagined that in five years Mr. Muhammad's adultery, a corrupt NOI leadership, and a presidential assassination would be conspiring to silence Malcolm's voice and suspend him from his ministry.) Malcolm and I were still discussing NOI matters when we strode back into the hospital. We strode down the corridor. We strode into the waiting room. We waited. Eventually a doctor came down the corridor. He was looking for Malcolm. Malcolm stopped pacing. He discovered that he was the father of a healthy baby girl. He glowed, and whatever he may

have predicted or expected didn't matter at all. He gave the
baby the one name he had: Attila.

She was the spitting image of Malcolm. You could see some
of Malcolm's spirit in her eyes, and her face would light up
with Malcolm's wide smile. Whether Malcolm got that smile
from the Littles on his father's side or the Nortons on his
mother's I don't know. The reddish tint to his hair, though,
probably came from the Norton side. Malcolm really didn't
speak that much about his family, but he'd sometimes mention how his mother's mind had been broken by the hard
times in America's thirties and by his father's death at the
hands of white supremacists. Malcolm did not believe his
father was accidentally killed on streetcar tracks; he claimed
that a gag was in his father's mouth when the body was first
found. White supremacists and a white man's economy,
then, had finished what a generation earlier a white slavemaster had begun. Malcolm's mother had been born of mis-
cegenation, her mother having been raped by a white slave
owner. Malcolm bore his mother's color in his light skin and
reddish hair and maybe, too, in the gray shadows of his eyes.
He said sometimes he hated it. He hated the oppressor's
whiteness of it. Malcolm wanted his skin to be the same color
as his soul. Pure black.

I've known no one more purely or more proudly black
than Malcolm. He taught that pride to us all. Pride was what
he was teaching us in his lectures on self-discipline and self-
respect as well as in his personal example of continual self-
improvement. Pride lay in discovering our capabilities and
extending them, even with a hoarse throat. It lay in obeying
the law, in properly knotting a tie, in arriving on time. Pride
brought real hope to the birth of a child. Our pride was
black, and with Malcolm we learned to find it both in ourselves and in each other.

1964

At a press conference on March 12, 1964, when Malcolm X announced the formation of the Muslim Mosque, Incorporated (MMI), he stated emphatically that he would use the militant black nationalist mosque not "to fight other negro leaders or organizations" but to work with other civil rights activists to "find a common approach, a common solution, to a common problem." With that statement Malcolm openly entered the political arena which had been long closed to him by his affiliation with the Nation of Islam. He entered it, however, without the advantage, as yet, of a clearly defined program or plan.

For Malcolm discovery had proved for years to lie in the quest itself. In the spring of 1964 Malcolm's quest for his role as a Muslim leader in the struggle of twenty-two million African Americans for their civil rights took him many thousands of miles from Harlem. On April 13 Malcolm flew first to Frankfurt, then on to Cairo, and finally to Jedda. From there he set out on his pilgrimage to the holy Islamic city of Mecca. Profoundly moved by his experience in Mecca, Malcolm sent postcard greetings from the holy city to numerous American friends and associates, among them his collaborator on the *Autobiography*, Alex Haley. "I have eaten from the same plate with fellow Muslims whose eyes were bluer than blue, whose hair was blond, blonder than blond, whose skin was whiter than white," Malcolm wrote to Haley. "And we are all the same," he added. In a letter dated April 20, the FBI reported, Malcolm remarked that he had experienced a spirit of unity and true brotherhood with many of the white people he had met during his pilgrimage. That spirit had provided him with a new, positive insight into race relations, Malcolm continued, and had convinced him that in Islam lay the power not only to overcome racial antagonism but also to obliterate it from the heart of white America.

After his pilgrimage to Mecca, at the invitation of Prince Faisal, Malcolm spent nine days in Saudi Arabia as a guest of the state. On May 6 he flew to Nigeria, where he lectured at the University of Ibadan and appeared on various radio and television programs in the capital city of Lagos. The next week, in Ghana, Malcolm attracted huge crowds everywhere and lectured to especially receptive audiences, none more so than the enthusiastic students at the University of Ghana. Malcolm addressed the Ghanaian parliament on May 14, and the next day enjoyed what he himself described as his highest honor in all of Africa: a private audience with the politically progressive Ghanaian president, Kwame Nkrumah. In Ghana, as in Nigeria, Malcolm hoped to establish diplomatic ties between their black nations and the nation of blacks in America. With that hope, too, he traveled from capital to capital up the west coast of Africa, from Monrovia to Dakar to Morocco to Algiers, before returning to New York on May 21.

Malcolm returned with a beard and a plan. On June 28 Malcolm established the Organization of Afro-American Unity (OAAU), a non-Muslim organization that in time would prove to be multiracial as well as multicultural. The OAAU was conceived by Malcolm to alter the perception of the African-American struggle for freedom as a domestic issue of civil rights by placing it on the level of human rights. Ultimately, Malcolm proposed, the OAAU would take the United States before the United Nations for its systematic violation of the human rights of African Americans.

To forward his program and to initiate a plan of interna-

tional action, Malcolm again flew to Cairo, this time to attend
the African Summit Conference there. At the July conference
Malcolm appealed to the delegates of the thirty-four member
nations to bring the cause of twenty-two million African
Americans before the United Nations. After the second summit conference in August, Malcolm extended his stay in Africa to garner commitments of support from the African
nations. By October he had visited eleven African countries.
He had talked with their heads of state and addressed their
parliaments, but he had not so readily won their support.
Africa had strong economic and political ties to the United
States. Emperor Haile Selassie of Ethiopia was a particular
disappointment; a client of the United States, he refused
even to meet Malcolm X.

Malcolm had been gone a hundred and thirty-eight days
when he flew back to the United States on November 24. The
weather in New York had already turned cold and wintry.

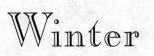

Winter

He knew that he was not going to die an old man. He knew, too, that time for him that winter was fast running out.

I remember a day not long before the end. I was walking with Malcolm from the Hotel Theresa to his car. It had been snowing. Malcolm was wearing a heavy, dark overcoat. He had pulled the flaps of his beaverskin hat down over his ears and a woolen scarf protected his throat and neck. Still, he shivered a little when he told me that he had been refused a life insurance policy because the company considered him too high a risk. Outright they had refused him; they had not even bothered with the formality of a physical.

Malcolm didn't try to hide his concern. He had no bank account. He had no money. The *Autobiography* had not yet been published, and he owned nothing else that he could sell. If he died uninsured, he would be leaving his wife and their four daughters penniless. "They refused to insure my life," he said. He paused, and I could hear the clink-clink of the metal clasps on Malcolm's galoshes as we trudged along the sidewalk. Malcolm had tucked his trousers into the tops of his galoshes. "That tells you how much my life is worth," he added.

The slush sloshed beneath our feet. "No, Brother Minister," I replied, "your life is invaluable to us." Malcolm smiled. In his eyes I saw the concern that included all of us, all his people.

His people were his mission. We were the reason Malcolm came back from Africa. He came back with hundreds of photographs from the many African nations he had visited, but in terms of beauty, no country had impressed him or his photographer's eye more than Ethiopia. "You know," he said one night when he was showing me the pictures he had taken in Africa, "if it wasn't for you all here in this country, I would have stayed there, in Ethiopia." His friends there had feared for Malcolm's life in America. They had tried to persuade him not to return to the United States. They had offered him a home there and the Ethiopian government had promised him sanctuary. Malcolm loved Ethiopia, but, he said, his mission did not lie there. It lay here, among us. "You are the only reason I didn't make Ethiopia my home," he said.

The autumn sunlight on the hills of Ethiopia had faded for Malcolm into a snowy, gray Harlem day. Bundled up in his beaverskin hat, a scarf and heavy overcoat, with his trousers tucked into his galoshes, Malcolm hesitated a moment at the door to his car. That day, like many days that winter, solemn thoughts weighed heavily on Malcolm's mind. He was haunted by uncertainty. It sat beside him every time he turned the key in the ignition to his car. It followed him when he brought his Oldsmobile to a stop at a traffic light, when another car—out of nowhere, it would seem—might pull up beside him and in a quick blaze of gunfire he might be dead. He knew his end was coming, but he didn't know how, or when.

Malcolm got in his car and turned the key.

Throughout the winter death threats to Malcolm arrived in the mail or over the phone. Assassination plots were frequently rumored. On the freeway in Los Angeles, in New York's Lincoln Tunnel, assassination attempts were initiated and failed. The Chicago leadership was calling for an end to the "scandalizing" of Mr. Muhammad by the hypocrite Malcolm X, and the Boston mosque, for one, was actively responding with plots against Malcolm's life.

The news from Boston was rarely good. Early in February Malcolm was planning to meet in Boston with Muslim sisters and brothers who had defected from Farrakhan's Mosque Number Twelve there. In New York, meanwhile, we received word that Muslim zealots from Farrakhan's mosque had plans of their own for Malcolm. Rumor had it that Malcolm would not be returning from Boston alive. Malcolm still wanted to attend the meeting, but we objected. Brother John and Luqman then volunteered me to go in Malcolm's place. For me, it was an honor.

I flew to Boston. Brother Busby met me at the airport and we arrived at the meeting without any incidents. It was held at the house of Malcolm's half-sister Ella Collins. I spoke with the brothers and sisters whose dissatisfaction with the national officials and sympathy with Malcolm had driven them from the Boston mosque. I thanked Malcolm's sister for her hospitality and then headed back to the airport with Busby and Malcolm's cousin in an old tank of a Cadillac.

It was late. Malcolm's cousin was driving. It was his car, it was his single-barrel shotgun lying at our feet in the back. I had noticed the new 1965 Lincoln earlier. It had pulled up along the deserted roadside and let us pass. Now it was beginning to overtake us. It passed us just as we were reaching the Callahan Tunnel. When we entered the tunnel, the Lincoln was blocking our path. Malcolm's cousin braked hard. Busby grabbed the shotgun. Four Muslim brothers from Number Twelve had left the Lincoln and were heading toward us when we screeched to our stop. Immediately Malcolm's cousin started backing up his all-steel Cadillac. The four Muslims lunged after it and were trying to grab hold of the door handles when Malcolm's cousin suddenly shifted gears. He gunned the Cadillac forward. He rammed the

shiny new Lincoln broadside, then backed up again. He had
thrown the four Muslims off their balance, but they were still
scurrying after us. I was grappling with Busby for the shotgun—he wasn't using it—when, abruptly, the Cadillac
jerked forward and slammed again into the Lincoln. The
next time the Cadillac attacked we practically tore off the
Lincoln's simonized fender. By then Busby had the shotgun
aimed out the window and the four Muslims were hightailing
back to their battered car. Malcolm's cousin reversed, advanced, rammed, and inched his Cadillac past the Lincoln.
We sped the rest of the way to the airport.

At the Eastern Airlines terminal Busby and I leapt out of
the car without even noticing that Busby still had a loaded
shotgun clutched under his arm and trigger finger. It was
eased away from him when we were apprehended by the
police inside the terminal. Someone had called the police and
informed them of an incident in progress at the Callahan
Tunnel; it's in an FBI report.

Someone had called the telephone company. The number I
had dialed, said the recording, had been temporarily disconnected. Certainly it had not been disconnected by Malcolm.
He had just left an MMI meeting and I had told him that I
would call to see that he'd gotten safely home. The recording
aroused all our suspicions. We feared for Malcolm's safety.

There were maybe twenty of us—Earl Grant, Brother
James, Brother Ivory, Calvin, Luqman, me, others—and we
decided to head that minute for Queens. In our bulky winter
clothes we crammed ourselves and our weapons into four
cars. We had all started carrying weapons that winter, for
our own defense and Malcolm's, so when we hit the toll
booths at the Triborough Bridge, four carloads of us, with
assorted guns pointing in every direction and rifle barrels
jutting out the windows, we must have looked like something
sent by Pancho Villa. We drove up to Malcolm's house on
97th Street in East Elmhurst. We knocked on Malcolm's

door. He answered it. He was all right. I told him what he himself had already discovered, that his telephone number had been cut off. He had also already contacted the telephone company. Their information showed that Malcolm himself had ordered the interruption of service, supposedly because he was going to be out of town for an indeterminate length of time. Malcolm corrected their information, and his telephone service was being restored.

Incidents like this did not help any of us to rest easier. Nor did Malcolm's weapon. All he had to protect himself and his family was a bolt-action rifle, the same caliber and make as the one Lee Harvey Oswald had used in Dallas. So that Malcolm would not have to pull the bolt back to eject the empty shell and then push the bolt forward to insert a new round, I insisted that he take my automatic rifle instead. I tried to convince him that an M-1 carbine with a thirty-round banana clip—it was much like the one I had used in Korea— would serve him better in an emergency. Malcolm agreed with some reluctance, but he agreed. We traded weapons.

That settled, I joined the brothers in their routine check of the neighborhood. That was when we detected the car parked about seventy-five feet down the block. Two men were sitting inside it. Our weapons raised, the twenty of us took positions on either side of the lamplit street. We motioned for the car to pull forward. Slowly it moved toward us. Slowly it advanced between our two columns. Then we roadblocked it. We discovered the two men were police officers who had been assigned to monitor the area and to provide Malcolm and his family protection. Malcolm knew nothing about it. We let the two officers pass. They waved as their unmarked car gathered speed and disappeared into the city's streets. A few minutes later we were heading back to Harlem. We left some brothers behind to stand guard outside Malcolm's house through the night. A quiet night, as it turned out, on Malcolm's block in Queens.

* * *

The block was quiet, too, the early morning hours of Sunday, February 14, and Malcolm's household lay in unsuspecting sleep. Then the firebombs hit. Around 2:45 A.M. the interior of Malcolm's house burst into flames that endangered the lives not only of Malcolm and Sister Betty but also of four children ranging in age from six months to six years. Malcolm angrily accused the NOI of the firebombing. The NOI, which held the title to 23-11 97th Street, in turn accused Malcolm himself of setting the blaze in order to gain publicity and to avoid eviction from the house by court order on February 15. Later, after thinking more calmly about the incident, Malcolm began to doubt the NOI's responsibility for the death threats and the recent actions against him. He couldn't believe that the NOI would in fact risk killing his wife and children in their attempt to kill him, or that they would risk killing innocent children, period. I may have shared his doubts then, but not now. I have been informed that there are recordings on tape of a former NOI official from the New York mosque actually bragging about issuing the orders for the firebombing to Number Seven's FOI. Malcolm, I think, wanted to believe that the evil of the NOI against him knew a limit. But it didn't. They would not have hesitated to burn down his house even at the cost of his family's lives. Muslim zealots could be so blinded by their allegiance to the NOI, I think, that they would not only commit arson but also, in their fanaticism, blindly violate Islamic laws that in fact protect the lives of women, children, and the elderly. To set fire to a house inhabited by innocent children is not Islamic; it's Satanic.

Muslim zealots in the FOI are capable of any act that they believe is justified by the Nation. The Muslims who tossed the firebombs through the windows of Malcolm's house, like those who had attempted on several occasions to assassinate Malcolm and like those who would eventually succeed, all believed one hundred percent that Mr. Muhammad had been taught by God and spoke for Allah. They believed that

America would be destroyed by Allah in Mr. Muhammad's lifetime. They believed that after Armageddon the faithful would be led by Allah's One True Messenger out of this place into the Promised Land and that the planet would then belong to Islam: The Nation would rule the Earth. They believed that Fard was God. They believed that Mr. Muhammad would not die. They believed without doubt or question that Malcolm was a hypocrite, a speaker of lies and rumors about their infallible, morally flawless leader, and they had been taught to kill the hypocrite wherever they might find him. That they themselves might be killed in fulfilling their mission would not in any way dissuade them, for they had been given a sacred cause. They had been called upon by the very top officials in the NOI whose leadership they devoutly honored and whose orders they eagerly obeyed. Neither the FBI nor any other federal agency or criminal organization had to contrive Malcolm's assassination. The NOI did it for them. Ultimately the NOI had Malcolm killed not for spreading lies but for speaking the truth, as he did when he told Mike Wallace about Mr. Muhammad and the secretaries on national television. Only in death could the NOI finally silence Malcolm X.

The silence fell on February 21, a Sunday, at an OAAU rally in Harlem's Audubon Ballroom. Malcolm's promise earlier in the month that he would present the OAAU charter at the rally on the twenty-first was attracting a good-sized crowd that afternoon. It was a mixed crowd, too, much of it non-Muslim. Malcolm had directed the MMI brothers at the rally not to carry weapons that particular Sunday because, he said, he didn't want to alarm the non-Muslims in the OAAU membership and he didn't want any of the more trigger-happy Muslims among us starting any incidents on this important occasion. At least one of the brothers, Reuben X Francis, disobeyed; he concealed a .45 pistol on himself when he came into the meeting. Malcolm had also instructed us not to check the person of anyone attending the rally for weapons or alcohol. "Anyone who comes, let them in," he had told us. Anyone who came that aroused the suspicions of the MMI brothers, however, would have been checked, despite our instructions, so as to ensure Malcolm's well-being.

The rally was late getting started. Both the Reverend Dr. Galamison, a civil rights activist, and Ralph Cooper, a popular disk jockey and well-known talent scout with ties at the Apollo Theater, had been booked by the OAAU secretary to open up the rally. It was nearing two o'clock, and neither of them had shown up as yet at the Audubon. Nor had the singing group that Cooper had planned to try out before a Harlem audience that day. Unpunctuality upset Malcolm. Unmet commitments upset Malcolm, and not only had Cooper and Galamison failed to appear but also Malcolm's drafting committee had failed to complete the OAAU charter. So Malcolm was already upset when Brother James came backstage to tell Malcolm that Ralph Cooper had called to say that he couldn't make it. Still, I would never have predicted Malcolm's reaction. He exploded. Why hadn't Brother James told him immediately, he wanted to know, and when Brother James said he had tried to reach Malcolm at home and had left the message with Sister Betty, Malcolm flew into a blind rage. After screaming at Brother James that he should know better than to tell Sister Betty anything, Malcolm burst out at all of us. "Get out!" he bellowed. "Everybody! Get out!!"

Only one time before had I seen Malcolm truly angry, the day he discovered that John Ali had misappropriated the New York mosque's funds, but even then he had not so totally lost his rationality and composure. Nor had I, until that gray February afternoon, seen Malcolm more distraught than he had been upon learning of Mr. Muhammad's infidelities, when he had felt as if his brain cells were bleeding. A sense of terrible foreboding had overcome me backstage at the Audubon. Neither singly nor together could Galamison's failure to appear or Cooper's cancellation or the unfinished charter fully explain Malcolm's behavior. God, we are told, does not burden a soul with more than it can bear, but I had thought as I'd stood there before his fury that Malcolm's soul could not bear much more. A metaphysical weight, it seemed, was sitting heavily on his back and shoulders. I felt the weight myself, on my own shoulders, but I knew it did not lighten the burden for him. I didn't know, either, what could.

Some minutes after Malcolm's outburst, the OAAU secretary came looking for me. She told me that Malcolm wanted me to open up the rally.

"How are you going to open up?" Malcolm asked me for the first time in the eight years that I had been assisting him.

"How do you want me to open up?" I responded, surprised that he had not said, as he usually did, simply to follow my own mind. Then I suggested that I prepare the audience for his announcement regarding the failure of his committee to complete its draft of the OAAU charter. I said that I would speak about voyages and the disappointments we experience when unexpected circumstances prevent a ship from reaching its destination on time. As I spoke to him, though, I thought that I was looking at a man who could voyage no farther, a man who had come to a dead stop and could neither turn back nor move forward. He could only stand there beneath the weight of his overburdened soul.

"Okay," said Malcolm. "Make it plain."

I looked into Malcolm's face. Again I felt the heaviness in his soul bearing down upon me. It lay upon me with such weight that I thought I couldn't even move my feet. I felt dazed, I wanted to perspire. Unsteady, I made my way to the podium onstage at the Audubon.

I talked about a ship voyaging the Atlantic. I talked about ocean storms that it sometimes rode and that other times it had to circle. I talked of trade winds and doldrums, of the many unforeseen delays that might keep even a well-captained ship from arriving in port at its scheduled time. I talked about Columbus who asked for the Great Khan of China when he landed another entire continent and ocean away from the destination he had charted. When I finished, the weight seemed only heavier on my shoulders, and under my suit I could feel the perspiration rising on my back. I turned away from the podium.

I was going to take the stage chair that Malcolm had been sitting in, but he stopped me. He put his hand on my arm and spoke into my ear. He instructed me to go to the green room just offstage and to have Brother James and the OAAU secretary inform him the minute that Reverend Galamison arrived. Somewhat perplexed—it seemed apparent to me that Galamison would not appear—I left the stage. As I stepped into the green room I felt beads of perspiration beginning to dampen my forehead. I shut the door behind me before telling James and the secretary what Malcolm had said. Then I sat down. I heard a sound like firecrackers, I heard panic, I heard blasts of gunfire—all in a matter of seconds. The perspiration broke out of every pore in my body. I knew that he was gone.

I knew that he was gone even before the door from the stage to the green room burst open and someone came running through. I just sat there, stunned, staring through the open doorway at the body on the stage. I couldn't move. Malcolm was lying on the floor of the stage, his face up, and I thought for a moment that he was trying to breathe, but his eyes were fixed—it seemed almost that they were fixed on me—fixed and unblinking; and I couldn't move. Then, all at once, it left me, the weight on my shoulders, and I felt a great relief come over me, Malcolm's relief from all his suffering. Death ends a thing on time. Whatever may be the instruments to bring it about, when it comes, it comes on time.

How long I sat there I don't know. When I got up from the chair in the green room and walked back out onto the stage, everyone had left the Audubon. My eyes scanned a deserted ballroom, an empty stage, the podium, the microphone, an overturned chair. On the floor of the stage I noticed a ring. I picked it up. The onyx stone was inscribed with *Allah* in Arabic. It was Malcolm's ring. A bullet had shot it off his finger. I put it in my pocket; later I gave it to Sister Betty. I stood at the podium. The microphone was dead and my mind was as vacant as the place. I didn't even wonder what time it was.

We had started late. It was after two o'clock when I began the opening. I spoke for twenty or maybe twenty-five minutes, so it must have been close to three o'clock when Malcolm offered the audience his salaams. Just as he was about to begin his address, a man near the center of the audience started a commotion. Pushing back his chair, he leapt up and said loudly to the person next to him, "Nigger, get your hand out of my pocket!" On top of the accusation, from the same area, came a few rapid shots that sounded like firecrackers. "Hold it!" Malcolm shouted from the podium; you can hear it on the tape of the rally. "Hold it!" he shouted into the blasts of gunfire not fifteen feet away from him. A bullet cut through Malcolm's microphone. He reeled back, he fell. It had happened in a matter of seconds.

The audience had panicked. Chairs were flung helter-skelter across the ballroom as three hundred people, most of them screaming, scrambled for the door. Another hundred ran blind. Some fell to the floor. Sister Betty swept her children under a table; her head down, she covered them with herself and her coat. A Muslim audience would not have panicked. It would have responded to the situation with military discipline, not like a herd of cattle in a thunderstorm. Had the audience not stampeded, the Muslim brothers who were present could probably have taken all five assassins. Instead, Luqman ended up with a bullet hole in his coat after trying to stop one of the assassins by hurling a chair at him, and another brother got hit in the stomach. Reuben X Francis, however, had his .45. He wounded the one assassin who was taken that day at the Audubon—Talmadge Hayer, a member of the Newark mosque and a resident of Paterson, New Jersey.

Not until four or five days later did the police pick up Thomas 15X Johnson and Norman 3X Butler, both of whom were charged with murder in the case of Malcolm X. Neither Johnson nor Butler had gone with Malcolm when he left the Nation, so either of them could probably have been enlisted by the NOI to assassinate Malcolm under the Muslim code of honor. Neither of them, however, had attended the rally at the Audubon that Sunday. If they had, I would have spotted them from the platform when I was opening up. Luqman or any of the other brothers at the door would have recognized them if they had entered the ballroom. As any current NOI member was considered suspect by us, both Johnson and Butler would have been checked for weapons at the door and, in all likelihood, been barred from the meeting. (In March 1965 I testified both to the assistant district attorney and before a grand jury that as I had left the stage, I had not in fact witnessed the assassination and therefore had not seen the assassins themselves. I was nevertheless certain, I testified further, that neither Butler nor Johnson could have been involved in the assassination as neither was present that day at the Audubon. I stated, too, that in my view, the assassins were NOI Muslims but were not members of the New York mosque. Had they been, I pointed out, Luqman, James, I, or any of the other MMI brothers at the meeting would have recognized them. I was not called by the defense to testify at the trial itself.)

I don't know how Betty Shabazz or anybody else was able to positively identify the suspects Butler and Johnson and thus place them at the scene. Especially Butler. That Sunday morning, the very day of the rally, Butler had been in the hospital to have work done on his knee. Despite the fact that he couldn't have made the assassins' swift escape through the crowded, chaotic ballroom with his injury, Butler was indicted. Butler was incriminated mostly by his old tweed coat. That old tweed coat of his was the only coat I had ever seen Butler wear. Unfortunately for him, one of the assassins had decided to wear tweed that day.

From the outset both suspects denied the charges against them. When they came to trial the following year Talmadge Hayer testified under oath to the innocence of his two codefendants. All three were nonetheless convicted on March 11, 1966, of murder in the first degree. The case was closed. It stayed closed, too, when Hayer later named his four accomplices, all of them members of the Newark mosque and all of them duped, like Hayer himself, by their Muslim zealotry. Hayer had testified that he got ten thousand dollars for assassinating Malcolm X. I don't believe, however, that Hayer or any of them did it for money. They did it for the Nation. They were devoted, they had been given a sacred mission. Around three o'clock on Sunday afternoon, February 21, 1965, they accomplished it.

At 3:30 that dark Sunday afternoon Malcolm X was pronounced dead on his arrival at the Vanderbilt Clinic of Columbia-Presbyterian Hospital. His death made news for days in the press, on the radio, on television. You couldn't escape it. For days I could not pronounce the death that had emptied my soul. I couldn't eat, I couldn't sleep. I'd stay awake most of the night, then at five or six in the morning, just before sunrise, I'd find my way home and fall into bed. For an hour or so I'd drift in and out of shallow sleep while time, it seemed, unraveled inside my head. For weeks time seemed only to move backward, as everything seemed now to belong to history. I lived for weeks inside the cloud of my own grief.

In Harlem, at the Unity Funeral Home, I viewed the body of our Brother Minister. Wrapped in a seamless white garment, it lay in a modest casket. On the morning of February 27, still half in a daze, I attended the funeral services at the

Bishop Alvin S. Child's Faith Temple Church of God in Christ. Ossie Davis presided. In his eulogy he praised "our own black shining Prince," a phrase that for me did not capture the man I knew: the minister, from the Latin word for servant; our counselor, healer, judge, and peacemaker; the teacher at the blackboard with a world in his mind and a piece of chalk in his hand. After the service I went with the procession to Ferncliff Cemetery. A body in a modest casket was lowered into the ground.

A love died inside me that day. No longer could I bear love for all brothers in Islam, not for those who had conspired to kill Malcolm, or for Hayer and his four unknown accomplices who had been the instruments of Malcolm's death, or for the NOI officials in Chicago who had manipulated all of them by turning the minds of the Nation against its most admired minister. Those of us who had stood closest to Malcolm talked among ourselves of retaliation. We laid plots and we drew up strategies. Nothing ever came of them, not out of fear or inadequacy but out of respect for Malcolm himself. Malcolm would have preferred justice.

The courts denied Malcolm his justice. They convicted three codefendants but, I believe, only one assassin. Four other men with Malcolm's blood on their Muslim souls went free. The police, the FBI, the district attorney, the court, they all wanted a quick conviction and got it. They tied their case up fast. They preferred expediency.

On February 25, 1975, the day before Saviour's Day, after another long, debilitating bout with acute bronchitis, the Dear Holy Apostle, Messenger, and Honorable Elijah Muhammad died at Cook County Mercy Hospital in Chicago. The attending physician is reported to have commented that with his condition Mr. Muhammad should have been dead twenty years ago.

After his father's death W.D. (Wallace) Muhammad assumed the leadership of the Nation of Islam. True to his moral principles and to the memory of Malcolm X with whom he had shared them, Wallace made sweeping changes in the national leadership as well as significant ones in NOI doctrine. He changed the name of his father's organization to the World Community of Al-Islam in the West (it later became the American Muslim Mission) and brought it within the compass of traditional Islamic teaching. Whites were admitted into the mission's membership.

A black Muslim movement did continue, however, and the old name did not die. In 1975 Louis Farrakhan, who had become the minister of New York Mosque Number Seven after Malcolm's death a decade earlier, broke with W.D. Muhammad and established his own Nation of Islam. In addition to the name, Farrakhan also retained much of the essential spirit and black nationalist dogma that had defined the NOI for the past forty-five years. Discontent among old

NOI factions inside Farrakhan's new organization produced other splinter groups. One was headed by John Ali.

In 1975 Benjamin Goodman returned to the Muslim brotherhood under the leadership of W.D. Muhammad. After serving for three years as an assistant minister in the Chicago mosque, he was assigned his own ministry in 1978. Honored by W.D. Muhammad with the name Karim, he returned to Virginia. The American Muslim Mission in Richmond lay about eighty miles and thirty years away from quiet Suffolk's shade trees and unpaved streets, from backyard vegetable patches, freshly laid eggs, Easter Graded, and Mr. Nichols's general store. Benjamin Karim's memory had grown large and full since those days. Eight years inside the temple with his teacher and friend Brother Minister Malcolm had also made it grow rich.

Index